Ventura County
LOOKING BACK II
GROWING A COUNTY: THE DEPRESSION THROUGH WWII - A PHOTOGRAPHIC HISTORY

Presented by:

VENTURA COUNTY

STAR

Acknowledgments

This book was created through the collaboration of the Ventura County Star and the Museum of Ventura County. Instrumental in its realization were Star Marketing Director Monica White, Project Editor Andrea Howry, Star Copy Editor Don Scott, local historian Richard Senate, longtime county residents John Yeto, Gene Thrift, Lawanna "Cookie" Timberlake Tierney, and the Saticoy Coffee Gang, several longtime Ventura County residents who have met for coffee on weekday mornings since the early 1970s. The Star would also like to thank David Schmaeling and Donna Naten of Proforma Color Press, the distributor of this book, for their tireless assistance. Special thanks to the Museum of Ventura County Research Library for help in retrieving and identifying all the photographs used in this publication and allowing The Star to reprint these historical images of Ventura County so they can be shared again and again.

Above: An aerial view of Ventura and beyond, 1948. #2092

Copyright© 2007 · ISBN: 1-59725-119-4

All rights reserved. No part of this book may be reproduced, stored in a retrieval system or transmitted in any form or by any means, electronic, mechanical, photocopying, recording or otherwise, without prior written permission of the copyright owner or the publisher. Every effort was made to include a wide sampling of Ventura County history and to correctly identify each photograph. We regret any omission or misidentification. All captions and photographs used with permission. Published by Pediment Publishing, a division of The Pediment Group, Inc., www.pediment.com Printed in Canada.

Table of Contents

6 Surviving the Depression	70 Serving the Public
14 Building a County	84 Coping with Disaster
28 Tapping Oil Riches	100 Facing War
32 Harvesting the Bounty	124 Enjoying Life
38 Making Movies	142 Viewing Our Past
46 Expanding an Economy	154 Index

The Museum of Ventura County

Clockwise, from top: Rain on Bellas Artes by John C. Lewis (photograph); R. E., electronic jacquard tapestry by John Nava; Lakota Warrior, George Stuart Historical Figure®; Children from Willow School grinding acorns like the Chumash did; Luster Fish ceramic by Beatrice Wood; Chumash basket with lightning design.

The Museum of Ventura County is an independent nonprofit founded in 1913. Today it promotes understanding and preservation of the art and history of this county, from the time of early Native Americans to the 21st Century.

The museum serves more than 65,000 people a year, with an unparalleled collection of more than 30,000 works of art and historical artifacts. The Research Library holds over 150,000 documents and images. In addition to art and local history exhibits and programs, the museum displays its renowned collection of George Stuart Historical Figures®.

The museum is now in the process of a major expansion which will double its size, allowing it to increase its programs and services to Ventura County's evolving communities.

The number accompanying each photographic image in this book corresponds with its catalogue number in the Museum of Ventura County's Research Library. The Research Library is a noncirculating, special collections library, open free to the public Tuesdays through Fridays, 10 a.m. to 5 p.m. and on Saturdays from 10 a.m. to 1 p.m. It is located in the Museum of Ventura County, 100 East Main Street, Ventura, CA 93001; www.venturamuseum.org; (805) 653-0323.

MUSEUM OF VENTURA COUNTY

Foreword

Throughout the Great Depression, the war years and the postwar boom, Ventura County went through significant changes. Many had a lasting impact and continue to weave their way through the fabric of the county today.

Although the ravages of the Depression did not hit Ventura County as hard as other parts of the country, they affected the county in subtle ways. Thanks to the strong influence of agriculture, the county eased its way through this difficult period, and then, along with the rest of the country, went to war against one of the greatest evils - the Axis powers - the world has ever known.

The war demanded hardships and sacrifice from almost everyone, but no group was asked to do more than Japanese-Americans. With their families interned in isolated camps, young Japanese-American males from Ventura County fought with bravery and distinction, their units suffering huge casualties in some of the war's fiercest battles.

With the war won, the county, as well as the rest of the country, was on the move. From 1931 to 1944, the county's population grew from 54,976 to 75,313, then skyrocketed after the war to 104,000 by 1949. New businesses — entire new communities, in fact — would spring up, creating a robust and dynamic economic climate.

There were other hardships during this period. Floods, fires and other disasters plagued the county, taking a heavy toll in human lives and property. Ventura County residents proved resilient, rebuilding after each tragedy.

Not all was hardship and sacrifice. Much of the county remained bucolic as the decades passed, guided by the rhythms of a simpler time and lifestyle. There were celebrations big and small with festivals, parades and rodeos cementing the county's ties to agriculture and the West.

All of this and much more is captured in the pictures and words of this book. The pictures were generously supplied by the Museum of Ventura County. You may notice a large number of photos from the western portion of Ventura County as the majority of the museum's collection reflects this area. The museum encourages donations of any materials representing the eastern section of Ventura County to its Research Library. In addition, many of the words come from the pages of the Ventura County Star and its earlier incarnations. To eliminate confusion, all references to the newspaper are under The Star.

We are pleased to offer this look back at Ventura County's past. We hope this book is as entertaining as it is informative. We also hope that it enhances our appreciation for this remarkable, beautiful county.

Joe R. Howry
Editor and Vice President
Ventura County Star

Left: This photograph was taken one mile west of Ventura on the highway to Santa Barbara looking toward the Ventura River Bridge, 1926. #19300

Right: Three FJ-3 Furies ready for takeoff at the Naval Air Missile Test Center, Point Mugu. The planes were used as chase planes in missile testing operations at the center. The Furies were equipped to destroy the missile should it become necessary. #20912

Surviving the Depression

The stock market crash of 1929 plunged the United States into the Great Depression, from which it would not fully emerge until World War II more than a decade later. State and federal work relief programs provided paychecks to many who would otherwise have nothing, and Ventura County would reap the benefits of those labors with new and improved roads, bridges, schools and hospitals. The pistol range in Ventura, Balcom Canyon Road, Santa Paula's fire station and post office, the stadium at Ventura Junior College – later to be known as Larrabee Stadium at Ventura High School – and thousands of dollars' worth of repairs to county roads damaged by March 1938 floods were among the projects that put Ventura County on the road to progress and men back to work.

Shielded somewhat by a booming oil industry and agriculture, the county was slow to feel the impact of the stock market crash. "Wealth Rolling Into The County," read a Nov. 8, 1929, headline above a front-page editorial extolling the county's economic progress and seemingly promising future. Yet four months later, The Star announced it would run all help-wanted ads free for the rest of the month. "Let's Try To Bring Jobs And Jobless Men Together," the March 11, 1930, headline read. "The percentage of people out of work here is much less than in many places," the story stated, "yet it is large enough to constitute a serious problem."

Left: *Bean threshing in Ventura County, Sept. 26, 1931. Former Managing Editor Joe Paul Jr. reminisced in a June 5, 1974, Star column about growing up during the Depression. "Living in a rural area such as this had its advantages in Depression days," Paul wrote. "It was possible to grow some garden items, but it was also possible to 'glean' fields and orchards after the harvests, and if your father happened to be a separator man on a bean threshing outfit, there was always a sack or two of limas."* #8377

Right: *Ted Iverson's children at home on Torrey Hill, Piru, 1931. Youngsters learned practicality in those days, Paul wrote. "Smarter kids during those low-budget days got wise about one facet of going to the movies: If you reported to the head usher that you had left a jacket or sweater in the theater the day before, you were allowed to go to an upstairs room where lost and found items were kept, and you could pick whatever fit you. By making a mental list of other items you saw in the collection, you could get them via another usher on another day."* #10282

Ventura County: Growing a County

Rags to Riches: Work camps for single, destitute men were established in several rural areas of the county – Matilija Canyon, Piru, Somis, Piedra Blanca. Hundreds of men from all over the country came and went, but none had a story like that of John Quincy Adams, a grandnephew of the second president of the United States. He was 67 and working as a baker at a camp on Toland Road just east of Santa Paula when The Star told his story on Jan. 23, 1936. Adams was earning a meager living baking bread, pies and pastries for the 200 men in the camp, but he was also just biding time until his uncle's estate settled. His inheritance? A cool $3 million.

Above: Ojai Fire Station, 1936, a WPA project. #2650

Right: John Palo-Kangas, the Scandinavian sculptor of the Father Junipero Serra statue, is shown with his wife and Van Esse, an expert in concrete molding. The federally funded arts project in front of what was then the Ventura County Courthouse, now Ventura City Hall, was unveiled on Nov. 27, 1936, by Gov. Frank F. Merriam. "The padre witnessed a surprising change in the place he once knew," waxed The Star that day. "Now he stood amazed to see great buildings and automobiles and thousands of persons – components of a modern, progressive San Buenaventura." Unfortunately, the statue's unveiling lost its lead-story position to other breaking news: "Roast Turkey Starts $15,000 Fire Here," the banner headline screamed. "Bakery Shop, Shoe Store Gutted." #17086

Above: The 1930 Ventura County Fair, of which this farm display was a part, would be the last for a decade due to a lack of funds. Clearly, it was missed. "Fair Attendance Mark Smashed," read the Oct. 10, 1940, headline. More than 11,000 people attended opening day that year, compared to 816 in 1930. #3557

Seafood: It helped to live near the ocean during the Depression. The beaches offered free recreation, and the Pacific yielded free fish and shellfish. The Dec. 9, 1935, Star told the story of one remarkable Mack Selby and an even more remarkable 2,500-pound Cuban bone shark that Selby harpooned from the Ventura Wharf. "According to observers, a school of the Cuban sharks was playing close to the wharf when Selby loosed a harpoon and speared one of the largest of the group. An air-filled tank was tied to the end of the rope and cast into the water. After a two-hour struggle, the shark finally gave up. Fishermen on an Associated Oil Company motor launch fired several rifle shots into the huge shark and towed it to the wharf where it was measured and weighed."

Above: A happy trio with their catch of halibut after fishing off a local pier. #10074

Left: Men enjoy a day fishing on the beach near Hueneme, circa 1940. #34965

Right: A man proudly displays his catch of the day, a large halibut, on the pier in Ventura, circa 1930. #10110

Ventura County: Growing a County

Above: Pierpont Bay, July 26, 1931. #3500

Art Critics: Gordon Grant's mural project in the Ventura Post Office at 675 E. Santa Clara St. was painted in 1936 as a federal arts project, but it wasn't without controversy. Depicting industries, resources and commerce typical of Ventura County, it was painted in what was called the American Scene Painters or Regionalists style. "Nearly all the workers look alike in form and facial features," explained the San Buenaventura Historical Preservation Commission's report of 1977. "This new style was not accepted by many local persons, and Grant found himself under very severe criticism. However, he has always been defended by artists who understand the style." The mural project underwent extensive restoration in 1966 after being damaged during a remodeling of the Post Office and was declared a historical landmark on Oct. 27, 1977.

Above: The Hotel Anacapa at Palm and Main streets in Ventura, 1930. On Jan. 7 of that year, The Star broke the news that the hotel was to be razed. "Modern Two-Story Building Will Go On Site," a secondary headline read. The story noted that the hotel's demise marked the end of an era, as the hotel had been built in the late 1880s during a building boom in Ventura brought on by the Southern Pacific Railway linking the town to Los Angeles. #265

Right: At more than 9 feet in height, the Serra Statue holds court over Ventura in 1940. Half a century later, the concrete had severely decayed, and the statue was replaced by a bronze version dedicated on Oct. 20, 1989. The 800-pound wooden carving used to create the molds for the bronze was put on display in the City Hall Atrium. The original concrete statue remains in storage. #19047

Ventura County: Growing a County

Building a County

Try to picture Ventura County without a Port of Hueneme, without sea walls along a nascent Pacific Coast Highway, without the comfortable climb of the Conejo Grade. Imagine bridges and piers washing out with every major storm and incredibly dangerous driving conditions year-round.

That would all begin to change in the 1930s, not only because such change was necessary with a growing county, but also because it put huge numbers of people to work.

In the Depression, such improvements gave people a reason to party. "Road Celebration Turnout Exceeds All Expectations," read a Oct. 23, 1933, headline. "30,000 Trek to Maricopa-Ventura Highway Jubilation And Eat Nine And A Half Tons Of Barbecued Beef."

Perhaps the county's greatest achievement during this era was the Port of Hueneme. From the time Sen. Thomas Bard announced his idea in 1867, the project was fraught with controversy and funding issues. Bard's son, Richard, took up the fight, and finally, thanks to a $1.75 million bond issue, construction began in 1939. "Hundreds Hail Harbor Ceremonies," read the Feb. 4, 1939, headline announcing the groundbreaking. The dedication, part of the Fourth of July festivities for 1940, was even grander, with a beauty contest, boat races, parachute jumping, fireworks and Goodyear blimp flights.

Above: *Port Hueneme, Livingston Aviation photo, Nov. 1, 1947.* #10618

Left: *Harbor construction, April 19, 1940.* #10651

Right: *Site of proposed Hueneme harbor.* #12145

Expect Delays: The Ridge Route, the main road between Los Angeles and Bakersfield, and the Maricopa Highway were arteries for the oil industry, so completion of the Maricopa and a redesign of the Ridge Route came as good news for many. In December 1929, the State Highway Commission decided to relocate 26 miles of the Ridge Route, the first of three major redesigns of what would eventually become Interstate 5. Not only would the project straighten some of the 697 curves across 36 miles, but it also would be a source of employment during the Depression.

The completion of the new "Conejo Pass" in April 1937 - a $550,000 project that took 17 months - was cause for a fiesta and parade. The new road was called a "safety link" because it eliminated the earlier road's treacherous curves. "The famous Conejo hair-pin turn was gone, superceded by a straight-line grade less than 7 percent steep," read an April 30, 1937, article. Alas, the very day after the road's opening, the new Conejo claimed its first fatality when a car plunged 300 feet off the side of the road, within 150 feet of what had been the speakers' platform.

Not all grand plans of the 1930s came to fruition. "Ventura Planned As West End of National Highway," read a Feb. 13, 1934, headline, describing a dreamed-of interstate that would end in New Hampshire.

Above: Taking a break from road work, 1930. #12007

Right: Working the Ridge Route, 1933. #12009

Below: Ridge Route workers camp. #12004

Building a County

Above: *Ridge Route morning crew.* #12005

Right: *Travelers stop to admire a rocky hillside as seen from Maricopa Highway on the way to Pine Mountain, Oct. 9, 1933. The road would open officially later that month.* #7364

Below: *View looking north on Maricopa Highway, showing part of Cuyama Valley, Oct. 9, 1933.* #7362

Above: These festivities celebrated the opening of the Maricopa Highway on Oct. 22, 1933. #18658

Left: View from Highway 1 looking north toward Point Mugu, January 1937. #15797

Right: Clearing the way for the construction of a sea wall along Highway 1, 1930. #15792

Opposite: Travelers to the 1933 Days of the Golden West celebration in Ventura take in the views from the spot where thousands of people would later celebrate the opening of the Maricopa Highway. Officials had already assured drivers of an unencumbered view. "Taboo Laid On Highway Billboards," read a Feb. 13, 1930, headline. "Maricopa Road Is Officially Made Scenic Boulevard By Commission." #7358

Above: Gov. C.C. Young cuts the ribbon to open Coast Road from Oxnard. Young was governor from 1927 to 1931. #26231

Before the Numbers:

Road work was constant along the coast. Sea walls were built, landslides were cleared, new names were given. "Board Puts Okeh On 'Pacific Coast' Highway Title," read a Dec. 15, 1931, headline, referring to the road that would eventually run from Baja to Alaska. The story cited one supervisor's concerns: "'Pacific Coast Highway is a suitable name, all right,' Supervisor Tom Clark said, 'but we can call it The Malibu among ourselves, can't we?'"

Above: *The American Sailor docks at Port Hueneme. The 10,000-ton training ship arrived in August 1941 and sailed to Pacific Coast ports on goodwill tours.* #10642

Right: *Local beauty queen contestants pose on top of a lumber carrier during the first Port Hueneme Harbor Days celebration on July 6, 1940. On top of the carrier are, left, Mary Grimm, who later became Mrs. Don McKenzie of Port Hueneme, and Cookie Timberlake, who became the wife of Cmdr. Glen Tierney of Point Mugu. Sitting above the tires are, left, Helen Abplanalp, who became Mrs. David Petit of Oxnard, and Meg Coleman, who became Mrs. Gene Hovley of Ojai. Standing in the center is Dora Peverley.* #10595

Below: *Wharf ship and sacks of cargo at Port Hueneme.* #26202

Above: *Sea wall along Highway 1 at Point Mugu, January 1937.* #15789

Opposite: *The Margaret Schafer, the first oceangoing cargo vessel to dock at Port Hueneme, begins to unload 490,000 board feet of lumber on Jan. 3, 1941.* #10626

Above: The Oxnard Harbor District dredges the port, scooping out to a depth of 30 feet. #7728

Left: Dedication of the harbor, 1940. The man in the center facing the camera is John Lagomarsino. #10588

Below: Preparing to move the Point Hueneme lighthouse, 1940. #26808

Above: View of Hueneme Lighthouse, circa 1939. #26811

Below: Woman with pennant at Port Hueneme. The lighthouse is on blocks, in preparation for the move. #26216

Above: The move turned into a media event and included a champagne bottle-breaking ceremony. #26212

Left: The lighthouse is raised, ready for moving. #26217

Moving the Lighthouse:
The historic Point Hueneme lighthouse posed a problem with port construction. A new concrete structure was being built to replace it, and the original was to be torn down. However, a yacht club stepped in to have the 125-ton structure hoisted 5 feet above the sandy soil, rolled onto a barge and shipped 600 feet across the harbor entrance.

Sensing a media event, Port Hueneme's new publicity chief sold the story to the national press on the fact that the 66-year-old building might not make it across the harbor. A photographer for Life magazine showed up for the February 1940 event, as did representatives of newspapers and newsreel companies. In the contingent that met them were six Oxnard girls who conducted a champagne bottle-breaking ceremony for their benefit.

Opposite: The lighthouse and moving crew at Port Hueneme, ready for the move. #26215

Left: The lighthouse moves across the bay on a barge. "Distance somehow lent enchantment and stature to the ancient building as it floated gracefully out into the early morning dimness," read the Feb. 17 wrapup. "As it cleared the shore, one newspaperman said: 'There goes the picture everybody wanted. And there isn't a cameraman on the scene.'" #3329

Below: The lighthouse at Hueneme sets off across the bay on a barge. #26805

The Media Event that Wasn't: The move did not go smoothly. "32-Hour Battle Unended," read the Feb. 16, 1940, headline that detailed the delays. "Three newsreel cameramen came yesterday, but left at dark," the story stated. At one point, the structure nearly broke free as it was being moved onto the barge - "a gosh-awful scare," the article called it - but an emergency cable averted tragedy. The barge was completely afloat at 3 a.m., but there weren't many around to see it. "Newspapermen and cameramen - with the exception of one Oxnard reporter and two Star-Free Press reporters - had given up their vigil after 5 hours," the Feb. 17 article stated.

Above: *A ship off the wharf of Hueneme.* #26201

Below: *Santa Paula Airport.* #20248

Above: *Construction at Santa Paula Airport.* #15524

Controlling the Skies, Rivers: Bridges, dams and airports were conceived and completed during the 1930s and 1940s. A large Fourth of July celebration in 1935 included the dedication of the Oxnard Airport, "considered one of the most carefully laid-out landing fields in the state," a July 3 story stated. Santa Paula Airport already had been in existence for many years, but in 1934, the 19 men who owned it asked the county to take it over. "Board Denies Santa Paula's Airport Plea," read the May 4 headline. The county rejected the $10,000 purchase, claiming insufficient funds and high unemployment. Matilija Dam was heavily criticized before its completion in 1948 and would remain empty for three years due to drought. Criticism never subsided; debate continues today as to whether it should be torn down.

Above: Hanging rock at Matilija Dam, 1948. #1593

Below: Matilija Dam. #10760

Above: Matilija Dam spillway. #5951

Below: Bridge construction takes place in the Point Mugu vicinity, circa 1940. This bridge crossed Calleguas Creek. #26661

Tapping Oil Riches

At the start of the 1930s, the oil fields along Ventura Avenue were among the most productive in the United States. "Avenue Yield Is 20,934,388 Bbls in 1929," read a Feb. 3, 1930, headline. By 1940, that had dropped to 12 million barrels, but fields in Santa Paula, Fillmore and the Rincon pushed up countywide production to 18 million barrels a year, according to The Star's Sept. 14, 1940, Progress Edition.

Records were constantly being set for the most oil, the largest rigs, the deepest wells. "World's Largest Drilling Rig Begins Work On Avenue," read an Oct. 3, 1931, headline. The derrick was 178 feet tall.

"World's Deepest Well Comes In Here," The Star reported on Jan. 19, 1937. The Avenue well was 9 feet past the two-mile mark. A few months later on the Rincon, Chancelor-Canfield-Midway Oil set a production record for that area when 1,964 barrels flowed in the first 24 hours at its B-13 well. "Record Rincon Oil Well 'In' For CCMO," the April 19, 1937, headline read.

Through it all, Ventura County prospered. "Shipped to all parts of the globe, the oil and gas and by-products from these wells return more than $30,000,000 in wealth to the county each year," stated The Star's 1940 Progress Edition.

Left: *An aerial view of a Ventura oil field, 1935.* #7796

Right: *Avenue oil field, 1935.* #3367

Ventura County: Growing a County

Right: Shell Oil employees in front of the old office building, 1939. #9235

Above: Standard Plant No. 4, May 1940. #8503

Left: Texas Co. Well #15 on Willard Lease on South Mountain, January 1930. #9959

Right: Oil drilling crew using newly patented wire line bit for drilling, 1927. #12127

Above: Anderson 19, 1940. #8492

Below: Anderson 8, October 1947. #8481

National Security: The Avenue's oil was so vital to the interests of the United States that on Feb. 23, 1942, when a Japanese submarine surfaced offshore from the Ellwood oil field north of Santa Barbara and opened fire, immediate attention turned to the security of the Avenue. According to the California Department of Parks and Recreation, the California National Guard set up two 155mm cannons on what is now Emma Wood State Beach, near the mouth of the Ventura River, and a mobile searchlight to scan the ocean. In October 1942, the 56th Coast Artillery Regiment from the San Francisco area relieved the National Guard and set up Camp Seaside at what is now the Ventura County Fairgrounds. Equipped with Long Tom guns that could fire a 94-pound projectile 14 miles, the unit practiced dry firing twice a day and, once a month, fired live ammunition at targets towed offshore. The targets were coordinated with spotters at Grant Park and on the bluffs above Seacliff. There is no record of any attacks on the Ventura oil fields; remnants of the gun mounts can still be seen at Emma Wood.

Harvesting the Bounty

"A Month On County Farms: 6,000 Men And $400,000." The Sept. 14, 1940, Progress Edition of The Star reported that although exact figures weren't available, farm labor was most likely the greatest source of work in Ventura County. In an average month, the paper reported, "approximately 6,170 seasonal workers will be at work in Ventura county fields, orchards and packing houses." Peak months were July through October, thanks to apricot pitting and drying, the bean harvest, the walnut harvest, sugar beet processing and the picking and packing of Valencia oranges. The steadiest work was in the lemon orchards. "Striking an average daily wage of $3 for farm hands, these figures indicate that the average monthly payroll for Ventura County farms would total nearly $450,000," the report stated.

As with oil production, agriculture set records year after year. "27 Million Dollars: Ventura County Crop Returns For 1937 Set All-Time Mark," read a Jan. 30, 1938, headline. "Citrus Income In Lead Again." Beans came in a weak second, at $3.5 million, compared to the $17 million generated by citrus. Growers continued to diversify: "Run through the agricultural alphabet from Apricot to Walnut and you'll find them all represented," stated the Progress Edition.

Farmworker strikes temporarily threatened the industry in 1941. Worker shortages did the same during World War II, leading the Farm Security Administration to import hundreds of Mexicans to work the fields. The effort paid off: Gross receipts on crops totaled more than $52 million in 1943, $17 million more than the previous year.

New Look: The agricultural work force changed during the early 1940s as men left for war. Women went to the packinghouses, and Mexicans worked the fields. An April 6, 1943, Star article with the headline "850 Imported Mexicans At Work On Farms In Area" reported that Farm Security Administration District Director M.E. Huffaker was pleased with the outcome. "Most of the Mexican nationals have never had previous citrus experience, but are proving adept at the work and learn readily, Huffaker declared. After the first week or 10 days, they 'hold their own' with old-time pickers, he said."

Left: Interior of lemon packinghouse in Santa Paula. #11731

Right: View south from Camarillo Heights, 1938. #26830

Ventura County: Growing a County

Field Work: Agriculture helped Ventura County through the Depression, putting hundreds of men to work in the fields and on packinghouse construction sites when relief funds dried up. Major crops, such as lima beans, had associations that held conventions, many in Ventura County. In 1936, several hundred California lima bean growers convened at Seaside Park for a barbecue, a boost to the city's economy.

Above: Bonita McFarland and Mr. and Mrs. Crane standing with a dog on the McFarland Ranch in Oxnard, 1932. #28464

Left: Men loading silage into a silo in Oxnard, 1940s. #34933

Above: Aerial view of corner of A and Ventura streets, Fillmore, circa 1937. #9693-83

Right: Men harvesting vegetables in Oxnard, 1940s. #34936

Above: Men work at the vats in the beet sugar factory in Oxnard. #9289

Left: Looking south-southwest from Gonzales Road at Oxnard and Port Hueneme, circa 1945. #26226

Above: Oxnard Citrus Association building, right, and Hueneme Recreation Center, circa 1940s. #34968

Right: Bean planting tractor, 1941. #2107

Right: Aerial view of the Oxnard beet sugar factory, 1948. #1265

Above: The one millionth bag of Crystal Brand Sugar, October 1950. #9300

Left: Man filling crystal sugar sacks. #9294

Right: Apricot harvest at Elliott Hendry Ranch, Moorpark, 1947. #14865

Making Movies

From the Philippines to the jungles of Africa to Shangri-La, Ventura County has played so many roles in movies that it deserves its own Hollywood star. The eastern portion of the county had proximity to the studios and a mountainous terrain that could become the backdrop for anywhere in the world. Western Ventura County had photogenic beaches and the Ojai Valley, both of which also became popular sites for movie stars' second homes.

To ensure privacy, much filming was done on private lands, such as Corriganville near Simi Valley. But once in awhile, the public was invited not only to witness the filming but also to become part of the movie. That happened in 1931 when Seaside Park became the venue for "Roar Of The Crowd," a name that was changed to "The Crowd Roars" when it was released the following year. "Movie Firm Coming Here For Picture," roared the Nov. 30, 1931, headline. The auto racing movie starred James Cagney, but it was racer Billy Arnold who drew the big crowds. They weren't disappointed – on Dec. 2, Arnold crashed through a fence and broke a rib.

As early as 1934, the county had recognized the economic potential of cinema. "It is estimated that thousands of dollars monthly are flowing into Ventura County from this new industry, which is assuming permanent proportions," a Feb. 9, 1934, article stated.

Left: David Niven and a leading lady, Andrea Leeds, on the set of "The Real Glory," filmed at Point Mugu. The 1939 movie, which also starred Gary Cooper and Broderick Crawford, had Point Mugu serving as a stand-in for the Philippines. The movie is described on the IMDb.com Web site as "A small American contingent tries to train rural tribesmen" to defend themselves against fanatical Muslim radicals in 1906 Philippines. #10123

Right: Clark Gable holds a couple of lion cubs at Goebel's Lion Farm in Thousand Oaks. #10583

Ventura County: Growing a County

Above: Filming of "The Real Glory" takes place at Point Mugu. According to the IMDb.com Web site, the dam destruction scenes filmed at Hunt-Salto Canyon near present-day Thousand Oaks had to be reshot, costing more than $10,000. #10097

Below: Goebel's Lion Farm became a landmark in Ventura County. In a May 1, 1978, oral history on file at the Museum of Ventura County, owner Kathy Goebel recalled how the animals would be leased out for filming and special events. "Every time they had a war bond drive," she said, "they'd call up for the elephants." The animals could cause a stir. "If you sit up at the wheel of your car some evening en route home from Los Angeles and count eleven elephants parading down the highway, don't worry for a moment," read a Feb. 9, 1934, story under the headline, "Drive Elephants From Simi To Movie Location." The elephants from Goebel's had been taken by train to Simi and driven "on the hoof" to Sherwood Lake for the filming of a Tarzan movie. Forty lions were also on the filming site. #10575

Above: Actor Gary Cooper hams it up during filming of "The Real Glory" at Point Mugu. #10104

Above: Louis Goebel, seated on the hood of his car, gazes at a favorite lion that leans toward him at Goebel's Lion Farm in Thousand Oaks. #14465

Left: Walter Northrup was the Lion Farm trainer during the 1930s. "He was a contract plasterer by trade," a 1985 Star article stated, "but there wasn't much call for his trade during the depths of the Depression." The camel, named Junior, was in "Road to Morocco" with Bob Hope and Bing Crosby. #9249

Jungleland:
Destined to become part of Ventura County lore, Goebel's Lion Farm, later to be called Jungleland, opened in 1926 on land now occupied by the Civic Arts Plaza in Thousand Oaks. It offered a home to the dogs, cats, rabbits and, most importantly, the five lions that were displaced when Universal Studios closed its animal farm. Later, according to a July 21, 1985, story in the Vista section of The Star, it would add giraffes, hippos and camels. The animals were displayed "for viewing and occasional petting" and were leased out to the movie industry.

Owners Louis and Kathy Goebel also would loan out the animals for charitable purposes. "Real Circus To Aid Church Fund," read a March 24, 1938, headline above a story detailing a fundraiser for a church in Thousand Oaks. Among the animals to be featured were Leo, the famous MGM lion; Prince, a tightrope-walking lion; and Queenie and Sally, who had been in the movie "High, Wide and Handsome."

Alas, Queenie and Sally would eventually meet tragic deaths. "Goebel's Swept By Crackling Flames," read the July 10, 1940, headline. Queenie, Sally, seven tigers and three camels died in a fire that was blamed on the spontaneous combustion of haystacks.

The Goebels sold the lion farm in 1946 and the name was changed to Jungleland. It went through several different ownerships, and the Goebels eventually bought it back. They sold it for the last time in 1969, and, according to the Vista article, auctioned off 1,800 animals "when Lion Country Safari siphoned off customers."

Opposite: Workers install palm trees on the set of "The Real Glory" at Point Mugu. Note the rock formation in the background, before Highway 1 cut through it and created Mugu Rock. #10095

Right: The lagoon side of Point Mugu, where the palm trees were used as movie props during the 1938 filming. #10084

Left: Actors and directors get ready for the next scene while filming "The Real Glory." According to the IMDb.com Web site, the movie, originally released in 1939, was reissued in 1942 with the title, "A Yank in the Philippines," but the Office of War Information requested that it be withdrawn; the Philippine Moros, portrayed as the enemy in the movie, had become allies of the United States during World War II. #10120

Above: A motion picture being filmed on location at Russell Ranch in the Conejo Valley. The movie industry has a long partnership with eastern Ventura County, from Tarzan movies to the television series "M*A*S*H." The Dec. 10, 1929, issue of The Star reported that Sherwood Forest, five miles west of Triunfo Canyon, was being used for scenes of "All Quiet on the Western Front." The movie about World War I would go on to win two Academy Awards. "A veritable 'no-man's land' has been constructed at Sherwood Forest, with barbed wire, blown-up homes and trees, wet, muddy fields, and all the trimmings," the article stated. #13448

Above: Joe Souza, Frank Whitlock, and Jo Neilson pose for this photo. Whitlock was the head of publicity for MGM until his death. #10103

Right: Point Mugu was used for other films in addition to "The Real Glory," the set of which is shown here. According to IMDb.com., in 1959, the television series "Men Into Space" was filmed there, as well as the 1960 John Wayne-Stewart Granger movie, "North to Alaska," and the 1992 movie "A Few Good Men," starring Tom Cruise and Jack Nicholson. Nearby Sycamore Cove was used for beach scenes in the 2004 Pierce Brosnan-Salma Hayak movie, "After the Sunset." #10597

Cinema Silver: Filming brought an economic boost to the area. Storms held up shooting of "Esquadrille" in early 1937, forcing the carpenters building the set near the Point Mugu fish camp to stay in local hotels longer than planned. "Mugu 'Battlefield' Soggy," read the Jan. 12 headline. "Rain Holds Up Work On Movie Set, Carpenters Staying Here And So Will The 'War' Stars." Once filming began, RKO Studios arranged for 100 people, including stars Miriam Hopkins and Paul Muni, to stay in Ventura hotels.

Left: Hollywood by-the-Sea, Oxnard. #26635

Expanding an Economy

Progress creates progress, and Ventura County of the '30s and '40s was no exception. Completed and improved roads brought car dealerships, mechanics and, after World War II gas rationing, fleets of buses. A growing population and a waning Depression meant more clothing stores, more utility hookups, more construction. A Dec. 31, 1935, article called business growth of that year "turning back the pages to the pre-Depression era," but it wasn't until 1939 that Ventura would experience its first million-dollar building year since "the boom days of 1929."

Beaches became a marketing tool. Hundreds of postcards showed sand and ocean and bathing beauties.

Unions came into their own during this time. The Star's Sept. 14, 1940, Progress Edition reported that at that time, 15 locals, all affiliated with the American Federation of Labor, were active in the county. "Unions Play Vital Part In County Construction," the headline read. Among those represented were the building trades, meat cutters and "motion picture machine operators."

Left: A Sunday beach crowd at Hueneme. #10593

Right: Beach beauties stretch out in Oxnard. #26230

Ventura County: Growing a County

Above: *A Ventura Beach scene looking east, July 1940.* #25215

Left: *Sunbathers and swimmers enjoying a day at Pierpont Beach, circa 1935.* #18676

Above: *Beach scene in Ventura.* #10378

Right: *Cars lined up near Pierpont Bay, July 26, 1931.* #3511

Frosting on the Cake:

Bill Baker's Bakery in Ojai became known nationwide thanks to its owner's marketing skills. In 1935, the bakery made headlines when a 100-pound fruitcake was sent to the White House. "Baker's Cake In Washington," read the Dec. 20 headline. The fruitcake was covered with candied roses and golden-colored taffy. The bakery also submitted cakes to county and state fairs and, in 1939, the World's Fair in San Francisco. Another specialty: lima bean toast.

Left: An employee displays a cookie tray in Bill Baker's Bakery in Ojai. #11702

Right: Employees take a break from their work to pose for a photograph inside the bakery. #11704

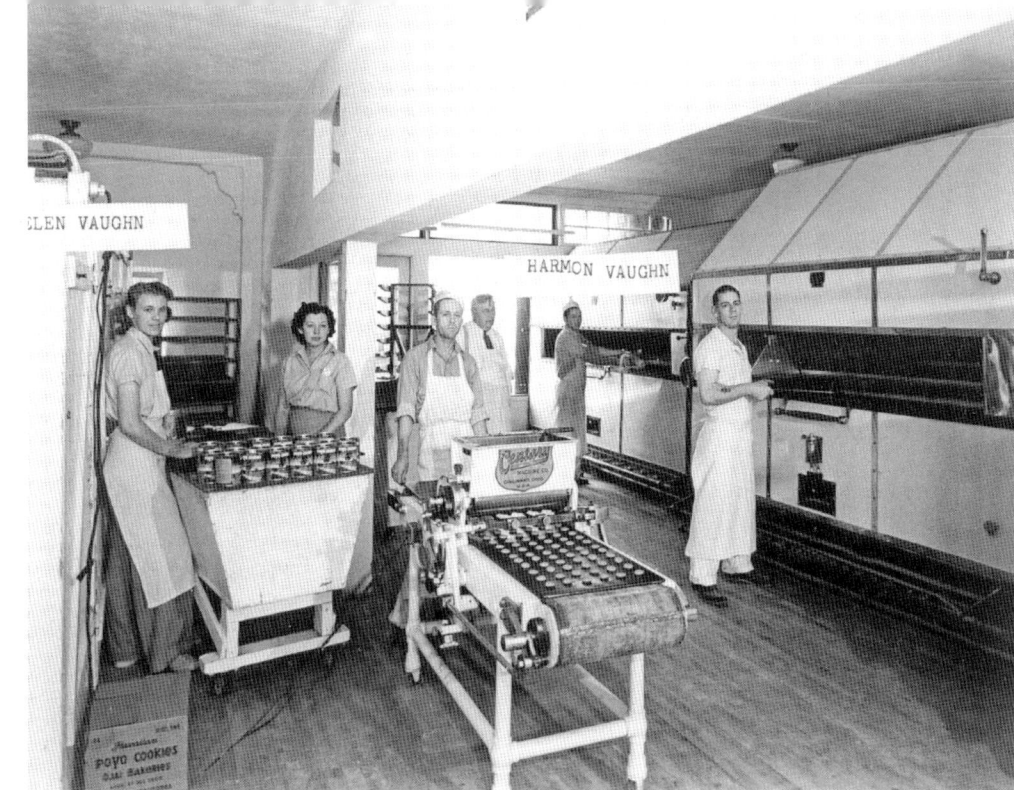

Above: Bill Baker's Bakery delivery fleet, Ojai. #11708

Left: Employees package (and sample) cookies inside Bill Baker's Bakery. #11705

Above: Papa Shima was a Japanese man who mended nets for catching anchovies at Point Mugu, 1937. #10109

[A]bove: Loading a freight car with boxes of Bill Baker's lima bean toast, Ojai. #11709

[R]ight: Anchovies at Point Mugu, 1937. The anchovies were [sa]lted and used when no fresh fish were available. #10106

[O]pposite: Actor and radio personality Joe E. Brown cuts [Bi]ll Baker's huge cake, one of many submitted through the [ye]ars at county and state fairs. Bill Baker is second from the [lef]t. #11712

Ventura County: Growing a County

Right: Hueneme Fisheries Co. fishing dock, Port Hueneme, 1940. #26802

Above: Hueneme Wharf and Warehouse Co., circa 1940s. #18116

Left: Fishing boats were plentiful at Port Hueneme. #10623

Above: The Ventura Theater building at Chestnut and Main streets was restored about 1950. It was built in 1928 in the Spanish Colonial Revival style. #7176

Above: Rose Hotel, Ventura. The grand hotels built when the railroad connected Ventura to Los Angeles in the 1880s were demolished to make way for more modern structures. Wreckers began tearing down the DeLeon Hotel on Nov. 23, 1933. Built in 1889, it had already earned "landmark" status in The Star article. #266

Left: Oxnard Canners Inc., on the north side of Port Hueneme, 1942. #11577

Above: The cottages at Foothills Hotel, Ojai, 1934. #8709

Above: The original Foothills Hotel, which burned in 1917. #4655

Right: The rebuilt Foothills Hotel, Ojai, circa 1932. #8706

Left: This Hobson Bros. Packing Co. truck was said to be the first refrigerated wagon in the county, circa 1931. #12528

Below: Ventura Pipe and Construction Co. with automobiles parked out front. #16906

Above: *View along the Ventura wharf and tracks, 1932. The old bathhouse can be spotted in the distance.* #7588

Right: *The meat department at the Inadomi Store in Oxnard, 1932. Standing from left are Dick Sakeda, an unidentified man, Salvador Ledesma and Cuco Flores.* #28441

Left: *Ventura aerial view, 1935, long before Highway 101 split the city. Note the courthouse at one end of California Street and the bathhouse at the other.* #7790

Ventura County: Growing a County

Right: Wonder Springs Water Co., 1241 Thompson Blvd., Ventura, 1933. #5997

Above: Tow truck at Joe Andrade's Garage, 42 E. Meta St., circa 1930. #9636-83

Left: Joe's Garage with Joe in the foreground, circa 1930s. #9635

Above: Marilyn Upham, the Ventura mayor, and a representative of Greyhound, December 1936. #7282

Above: Coca-Cola Bottling Co. employees are shown in this Feb. 26, 1938, photo. #17165

Right: Drivers pose with their trucks at the Coca-Cola Bottling Co. plant on West Main Street at Garden Street in Ventura, August 1935. #12107

Ventura County: Growing a County

Right: Lindenbaums' Emporium at 544 Oxnard Blvd. as it looked in the 1930s. #26598

Above: L.N. Diedrich Machine Shop in Oxnard, circa 1938. Farmers took equipment there for repairs. #26588

Left: The interior of the Jack Rose Smart Shop between Oak and California streets on the south side of Main Street in Ventura, circa 1938. The shop, founded in 1925, had moved to 434 E. Main St. in 1930. On its sixth anniversary, Oct. 2, 1931, The Star interviewed Rose. "Close personal service and up-to-the-minute fashions are the two factors which have contributed most to our success," Rose declared. #12137

Right: Roy Esaki with a fellow worker at State Super Market, Main and Palm streets, Ventura, 1938. #27512

Above: J.C. Penney store opening on the south side of Main Street in Ventura, December 1939. #12081

Left: Businesses line the 500 block of Oxnard Boulevard, circa 1938. #26599

Left: Hard-hat oil workers take a break for a photograph, February 1940. #7844

Right: The Pacific Telephone building at Santa Clara and Fir streets in Ventura, circa 1940. Utility hookups soared as the population grew. Just before the Depression hit, Pacific Telephone and Telegraph Co., which had established an exchange in Ventura in 1889, reported a gain of 426 telephones in the first 10 months of 1929. "Phone Company Hookups Large," the headline read. The hookups brought to 3,823 the number of phone service connections in Ventura that year. #18665

Above: The Oxnard yard of Peoples Lumber Co., circa 1940. #10945

Left: Peoples Lumber model house, circa 1940. The Sept. 14, 1940, Progress Edition of The Star noted that the company, which had formed on Sept. 13, 1890, had grown to 73 employees, eight yards, three mills and a monthly payroll of $12,000. A costly fire had taken a toll on the company a decade earlier. "$25,000 Fire Hits Lumber Yard," read the Jan. 24, 1930, headline. The nighttime fire, blamed on a faulty wire, destroyed the Fillmore mill and sheds and took three hours to extinguish. #10937

Ventura County: Growing a County

Above: A fleet of buses in front of Larrabee Stadium in Ventura, 1940s. #10317

Above: Weatherly Motor Company on Main Street in Ventura, circa 1940. #19900

Left: Marcella Wilson Anderson poses in a 1901 Cadillac in front of her father's business on the corner of Ventura Avenue and Main Street, August 1941. #12372

Opposite: An interior view of Meyers' Bakery with Charles Meyers, Oxnard, circa 1941. #26331

Above: Max Riave and his daughter in front of Camarillo Mercantile, circa 1945. #28096

Right: Four men pose in front of the Yellow Cab Co., circa 1948. Roy Weatherly is second from right. #18998

Above: Back of The Hub, a bar in Ojai's Arcade, circa 1950. #13479

Left: The interior of the Ventura Sportswear factory, circa 1940s. #10358

Above: A street scene in Ojai features an ice cream parlor, bakery and the office of a justice of the peace. #8263

Right: Display of lemons in Santa Paula. #11730

Above: Fred Hall at Topper Night Club doing nightly live remote broadcasts on KVEN from downtown Ventura, 1949. #16959

Left: Fans from Ventura High School are looking in on Fred Hall, who was at the controls of the original KVEN Studios in Pierpont Bay, 1949. #16956

Left: Joe Andrade's Garage at 42 Meta St., Ventura, and house next door. #9634

Right: Richard Siquedo drives this Hobson Bros. Packing Co. truck, a 1932 Ford. #12527

Above: An advertisement for a 1941 Pontiac available at McConica Motors in Ventura. #22297

Right: Oxnard Creamery at First and A Street and an ice company. #26593

Serving the Public

A growing population meant more schools, churches and hospitals, as well as stronger law enforcement. A higher value was being placed on education, and outbreaks of flu, tuberculosis and diphtheria forced county residents to recognize the importance of public health. But it wasn't just the growing demand that prompted the new schools, hospitals and sanitariums; their construction also provided work-relief employment.

Police and deputies dealt with everything from rumrunners to wild goose chases for John Dillinger and an escapee from Alcatraz Prison. "Woman Reports Dillinger Auto Was In Ventura," blazed an April 10, 1934, headline, three days before the bank robber raided an Indiana police station and stole several guns. The June 29 headline read, "John Dillinger Rumored To Be In The County." Stacked underneath were the headlines, "Officers Looking For Two Armed Men In Out-State Car; Pair Ask Road Out Of Valley; Informant Says He Saw Machine Gun In Their Auto." Dillinger was shot and killed in Chicago on July 23, and there was never any evidence he had been in Lockwood Valley or anywhere else in the western United States.

The same thing happened in December 1937, with reported sightings of Ralph Roe, who had escaped from Alcatraz Prison in the San Francisco Bay. He was never found.

Churches reflected the diversity of the population. Catholics built St. John's Seminary near Camarillo, in what was then a remote part of the county. Jeddu Krishnamurti began his annual talks in Ojai. Buddhists worshipped at their church in Oxnard. And a Baptist minister fought off a proposed nudist camp near Fillmore.

Left: *Students enjoy a maypole dance on the Oxnard High School athletic field. Many schools were constructed and improved during the Depression as work-relief projects, and they weren't cheap. When fire destroyed Fillmore Junior High School in 1937, the replacement cost was estimated at between $100,000 and $150,000. There were no fatalities in that fire; "No Children Or Teachers There," read a secondary headline on Jan. 21. School had been suspended due to a flu epidemic.* #26333

Right: *Ventura Police personnel, circa 1948.* #18805

Ventura County: Growing a County

Above: A local police force, circa 1940. #30550

Left: A policeman poses next to the Ventura School crossing sign. #10374

Above: Capt. Howard E. Marsh, California Highway Patrol, Ventura, beside his motorcycle, circa 1940. #12799

Above: Old Temescal School, Piru Canyon. #9019-83

Right: Plaza School, Fir and Santa Clara streets, Ventura, 1930. "Plaza Pupils Move To New Lincoln Structure," read a Nov. 13, 1931, headline. Plaza School was sold to the federal government for a new post office. #989

Left: Ventura Junior College, at Main and Catalina streets. It was also a senior high school, with 11th- and 12th- graders attending classes there. #7735

Below: Ventura County Free Library Bookmobile at May Henning School, 1949. #10383

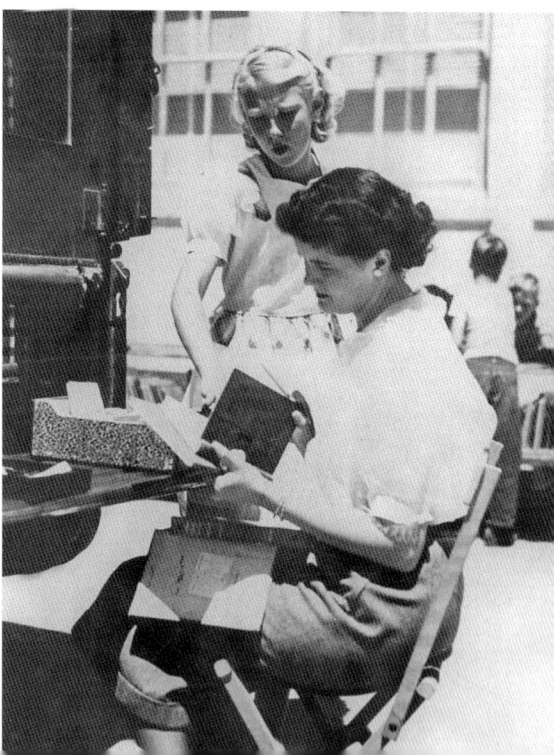

Teacher Pay: "Teachers Pay Is Increased," read a May 17, 1934, headline. The minimum salary scale for the Ventura Union High School District was raised from $1,750 to $1,800 per year. This followed the raise given to elementary teachers, who were now earning $1,500 a year, up from $1,350.

Nixing the Nudists: In 1934, led by the Rev. J.W. Jenkins of the First Baptist Church, Ventura Baptists began a campaign to prevent nudists from opening a colony at Pole Creek Canyon near Fillmore. "Pastors Charge County Youngsters Are Flocking Out To See Sights," read a March 1 headline. Within two weeks, the pastors' efforts had succeeded. "Nudists Seeking Another Site For Their Camp," read a March 12 headline.

Left: The old Congregational Church in Ventura, 1930. #8811

Right: May Henning School in Ventura, 1949. #10389

Above: Combined choir of old St. Paul Baptist Church in Oxnard and Olivet Baptist Church in Ventura, 1946. #25536

Left: The Rev. Jesse Walker and congregation in front of St. Paul Baptist Church on Seventh Street between B and C streets, 1944. #25539

Something for Everyone: Religion was as diverse as the county's population. On April 22, 1936, plans were announced that a new church for the Latter-day Saints would be built in the county. Two years later came news from the Catholics: "Plans For County Seminary Near Conejo Are Revealed," read the Jan. 10, 1938, headline. The March 20, 1939, dedication ceremonies of the $1.5 million St. John's Seminary - by now more accurately described as being "between Camarillo and Somis" - attracted 5,000 people. And each year, Jeddu Krishnamurti's lectures drew hundreds of people to the Arya Vihara estate near Ojai. "Krishnamurti Back In Ojai After Years In Far Places," read the May 10, 1934, headline. "Blames Troubles Of World On Men's Unwillingness To Think."

Left: The Rev. Taiken Masunaga and his family came to Oxnard in 1929. This photo was taken inside the Buddhist Church of Oxnard, circa 1930. #28237

Above: Children perform the Dojo Sukui dance at the Oxnard Buddhist Church, Oxnard, circa 1930. Miyoka Takeda is at left, Hiroshi Takeda is second from left. #27994

Right: Oxnard Buddhist Church Board of Directors, 1934. #27426

Right: This postcard, postmarked April 12, 1948, shows the Methodist Church in Moorpark. #21004.

Below: Camp Edna, a Girl Scout camp, was located above Matilija Lake; circa 1937. #14122

Healthcare:
From "tuberculosis preventoriums" to mental hospitals, healthcare facilities underwent tremendous expansion during this era. None was more impressive than Camarillo State Hospital, now California State University, Channel Islands. As the Sept. 14, 1940, Progress Edition reported, the hospital, "the newest in the state's chain of seven hospitals for mental patients," was its own city. Situated on 1,648 acres, it had its own farm, ranch, slaughterhouse, dressmaking shop, shoemaking shop, water plant and the largest sewage disposal plant of its kind west of the Mississippi. It was dedicated on Oct. 12, 1936, and by 1940, it had almost 5,000 patients and employees.

Above: Casa de Rosas Club, 1930. #10013

Right: The exterior of the Bard Sanitarium, which was built in the 1930s at Ventura County Hospital to care for 100 tuberculosis patients. This isolation ward was a work-relief project that was allocated $27,303. #14235

Below: Santa Paula Hospital. #20340

Above: A front view of the Ventura County Hospital on Loma Vista Street, circa 1930. On the hilltop behind the hospital stand the Five Sisters, five stately trees that served as a landmark and guiding post for travelers. Today, the spot is known as Two Trees, and a Nov. 1, 1940, Star article explained why. "Famed Trees Cut Down," the headline stated. "Three of the Five Sisters trees fell prey to a destructive Halloween gang during the night." #10521

Above: *Girl Scout camp at Lake Glenn, between Santa Paula and Fillmore, June 1934. Delee Staunton Marshall was one of the counselors for these girls.* #14119

Left: *In 1951, Ruth Gibson founded the Twentieth Century Onyx Club. She also worked at the Construction Battalion Center for 28 years.* #25533

Right: *The dedication of Pioneer Monument at Foster Park near Casitas Springs, June 1934. The plaque is now in front of the Museum of Ventura County.* #5070

Opposite: An undated photo of a meeting of the 20-30 Club, so named because of the ages of its members. A district meeting of the Club in January 1934 drew 70 members from the Central Coast to Ventura. #25090

Right: Delta Theta Tau Sorority installation, Pierpont Inn, Feb. 26, 1938. #11330

Above: A regional Boy Scout meeting, circa 1940. Tom Carr is seated far right. #18766

Left: Groundbreaking for a new fire station begins in November 1941. Construction of public works projects employed many during the lean years. "Huge Stride In County Building," read a Dec. 31, 1935, headline. Stimulated by work-relief funds, $2.5 million in construction took place that year, most notably the Ventura Pistol Range and Camarillo State Hospital. #18967

Right: Ventura County Grand Jury and Santa Paula Aero class visit Point Mugu, 1948. #15818

Below: Inspecting the charter of the Ventura County YWCA are, from left, Mrs. Fred W. Smith; Mrs. Bartlett B. Heard, national YWCA vice president; Mrs. Nelson Weed, Ventura County YWCA president; and Miss Myrna Weed. Mrs. Smith and Miss Weed were the first two purchasers of life memberships in the Ventura County YWCA. #8296

Above: The top floor of the Masonic Lodge at Santa Clara and California streets, 1945. The Masonic Temple opened to much fanfare in 1930. "New Masonic Temple Is Decorator's Masterpiece," gushed the Jan. 2 Star. "Grandeur Of Finishings Impressive To Visitor; Furnishings Are Elegant In Harmony." #836

Above: Miss Hope Gibson reads a story during summer story hour at the Ventura County Library, 1949. Education became a societal priority during this era. An Oct. 17, 1931, headline stated, "Illiteracy On Downgrade In County, Census Shows." In 1920, 9.8 percent of the population was considered illiterate. By 1930, that had dropped to 5.6 percent. By 1940, according to that year's Sept. 14 Progress Edition of The Star, the county had 50 elementary schools, seven high schools and a junior college. #10344

Left: Boys Club, Ojai. #13605

Ventura County: Growing a County

Coping with Disaster

Ventura County's three biggest enemies – fire, floods and heavy seas – took a toll during the 1930s and '40s, a time when residents were already trying to cope first with the Depression, then the eventuality of war.

While the natural disasters of this era would pale in comparison with the 1928 collapse of the St. Francis Dam, they were still expensive and destructive. Beach debris from storms damaged surfside homes and hurt a growing tourism industry; rockslides on the Rincon and Conejo Grade clogged the increasingly efficient road system.

Ironically, the worst storm of this period occurred 10 years to the month after the dam disaster and 33 years to the month after a devastating Ventura River flood, a fact duly noted in the March 12, 1938, Star headline, "Tale of Two Floods." The 1938 storms, which came in two surges, wiped out or badly damaged 20 bridges and caused $350,000 in damage to Ventura, Santa Paula and Ojai. It would also cost $25,000 to clear debris from the beaches – and create another work-relief project.

An earthquake struck Ventura at 11:53 p.m. on June 30, 1941, shattering windows and causing $6,000 in damage.

Providing some comic relief were the occasional snowstorms. Two inches of snow fell in Bardsdale and Fillmore, The Star reported on Dec. 14, 1931. "The children of both towns, many of whom had never seen snow at first hand before, had a gay time romping in it."

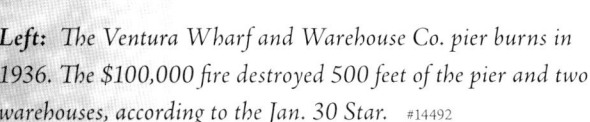

Left: *The Ventura Wharf and Warehouse Co. pier burns in 1936. The $100,000 fire destroyed 500 feet of the pier and two warehouses, according to the Jan. 30 Star.* #14492

Right: *A snow scene at Newbury Park, January 1949.* #15269

Ventura County: Growing a County

Above: The same day the Ventura Wharf and Warehouse Co. pier burned, Walter Chaffee, who managed the company for 11 years, died after a long illness, "unaware of the fire," the Jan. 30, 1936, Star reported. #14318

Left: Workers clean up from the pier fire. #14496

Left: Yards on Glen Ellen Drive in Ventura are covered with snow from a 1946 storm. Snow also fell in February 1939 and in January 1949. #17297

Right: Snow on the ground in January 1949, a rare sight for Port Hueneme. #15850

Left: Snow on a firehouse, Ventura, January 1949. #20685

Right: The March 1938 storms were considered the county's worst since 1914. Water roared through an underpass crossing in Oxnard during the subsequent flood. "County Asks Millions For Flood Relief," read a March 7, 1938, headline above a story detailing the devastation done to the county's road system. "The possibility loomed that several county highways, including roads through Matilija and Camp Comfort and the Bard bridge route from Ventura to Hueneme might be abandoned entirely." #3287

Above: The underpass crossing north of Oxnard on Roosevelt Highway during the flood of March 1938. #32

Right: A man inspects a flooded underpass crossing north of Oxnard in March 1938. #3289

Right: The March 1938 storms destroyed the main bridge between Santa Paula and Fillmore. A temporary bridge was built, but it washed out just one week after the main bridge was wrecked, according to a March 12, 1938, Star article carrying the ominous headline, "Further Rain Due Tonight." #10166

Above: Flooding in 1938 forced the evacuation of hundreds of people and left several dead, including two who lived in a shack at the mouth of the Ventura River and a Rancho Sespe worker who drowned in Howard Creek while trying to save a fellow worker. "Scores Flee Homes In SP, Ojai Valley," read the March 2 headline. "Relief Workers Feed Hundreds In County Areas," read the headline the next day. #10168

Left: Flooding in the Santa Clara River Valley, 1938. #10164

Right: Santa Paula Airport, 1938 flood. "Million Dollars Damage At S.P.," read a 1938 headline. Damage to residences was estimated at $500,000, while damage to public and commercial buildings and to farm lands was expected to total a similar amount." #10172

Above: Willard Bridge at Santa Paula during the flood of 1938. #10176

Left: A washed-out highway and railroad west of Fillmore, 1938. #10179

Left: On March 2, 1938, the Ventura River "burst its banks in four places and poured a flood of muddy water into the area," The Star reported. The main break occurred near the Seaside Oil Co. refinery in the Avenue area, shown here. "Thousands of cubic feet of water were pouring, streaming through Ramona and Sheridan Way streets. River street was under water," The Star reported. #10124

Above: Saticoy bridge washed out in high water, 1938. #17709

Left: Railroad bridge at Santa Paula. #10174

Right: Santa Paula Creek Highway Bridge, during the flood of 1938. #10173

Above: The Seaside Oil tank farm sits in the middle of a flooded Ventura River in March 1938. #8294

Right: Bear Canyon burning, as seen from Meiners Oaks Camp, September 1948. #17430

Below: The Ventura River rushes past Seaside Oil tanks and equipment in March 1938. #8295

Up in Smoke: Winter brings the rain; summer brings the fires. The 220,000-acre Matilija fire of September 1932 was the largest wildfire in state history until being supplanted in 2003 by the Cedar fire in San Diego County, at more than 273,000 acres. In 2007, it was nudged to third place by the 240,000-acre Zaca fire in Santa Barbara and Ventura counties.

Sixteen years later, the Ojai-Maricopa Fire burned 25,000 acres and 17 outbuildings, killing one man. Sparked by a malfunctioning butane tank at Wheeler Hot Springs, it was fueled by dry vegetation caused by a yearlong drought.

Above: Firefighters tend to a backfire in Senõr Canyon, now Senior Canyon during the Ojai-Maricopa Fire in September 1948. #17460

Above: Forest Service crew on the line at Gridley Canyon near Ojai during the Ojai-Maricopa Fire. #17372

Right: The Senõr Canyon backfire flares up on Sept. 14, 1948. #17373

Ventura County: Growing a County

Above: The surf is high on the old pier at Point Mugu. A new, higher pier was built in 1940 after the old pier washed out. #10088

Above: The old pier at Point Mugu. #10069

Right: High surf at Point Mugu, circa 1938. #10073

Above: The new pier at Point Mugu, circa 1940. #10096

Above: The old pier that washed out. #10075

Left: In September 1939, heavy seas wrecked the Point Mugu fish camp and destroyed wharves at both Point Mugu and Hueneme. Here, crews build new cabins for the fish camp. The Point Mugu pier was rebuilt immediately, but it wasn't until 1956 that another pier was built for the public at Hueneme, and not until 1967 was it made long enough for public fishing. #10094

Above: Pierpont Beach looking west from Seaward Avenue after the fishing pier was destroyed. #18675

bove: Fishing from Pierpont pier, circa 935. #18674

ight: California and Main streets in entura after a heavy rain in the late 920s. Note that the Serra Statue had yet be installed. #12446

pposite: A flooded Ventura venue. #10350

ier Pressure: A December 937 storm wiped out the Pierpont fishing er and took out nearly two-thirds of entura's pier. "Smashing Seas Leave Heavy oll Of Wreckage Along Beach," read the ec. 13, 1937, headline. Debris was found far south as Hueneme. The Pierpont er already had been condemned after beg ravaged by storms in December 1935.

Above: Fire at the corner of McFarland Drive and Ventura Avenue, 1947. General Machine Co. is in the background to the left. #15460

Right: The hull of the Coos Bay, which sank and washed ashore in 1915, is sometimes exposed when heavy seas batter the Ventura Pier. It happened on Nov. 25, 1947, and is shown here being inspected by workers. #15123

Plane crashes: The number of plane wrecks in Ventura County increased substantially during World War II as pilots in training took to local skies. Among them was a crash on Nov. 19, 1943, when a second lieutenant from North Carolina slammed his P-38 into a mountainside in upper Tapo Canyon north of Simi Valley in dense fog. Another P-38 pilot flying in the same formation was able to land in Santa Paula and survived.

One of the county's early air tragedies occurred on July 12, 1949, when a Curtiss-Wright C-46 belonging to Standard Airlines crashed into a rocky hill four miles south of the Santa Susana grade highway, killing 35 of the 46 people on board.

Left: Crash landing of an SNJ type aircraft, 1943. #15927-88

Above: Pierpont Beach, December 1937. #15457

Above: Pierpont Beach, December 1937. "'We Just Waited And Prayed,' Pierpont Bay Residents Say," stated a Dec. 13 headline. Damage was estimated at $171,000. Pierpont has felt nature's wrath numerous times. In December 1935, giant swells wiped out 150 feet of the Pierpont pier and wrecked a 40-foot Associated Oil Co. launch. Debris was scattered for two miles. The next month, giant waves took out 300 feet of boardwalk and 20 feet of a concrete sidewalk and damaged a two-story apartment house. Repair cost was estimated at $30,000 – and then the area was hit again one month later. #15458

Left: Windstorms also have taken a toll on the county. "Fires, High Winds Wreak Havoc," read an Oct. 23, 1935, headline. Not only did the winds knock down these telephone poles, but they also toppled a water tank on the Seaward Avenue bluff and blew it down the hill "where it was completely smashed." #30529

Facing War

World War II would forever change Ventura County. The military became a major economic force, establishing bases in the county and spawning a powerful defense industry. And, as happened in cities all over America, women joined the work force in droves, permanently altering social and family structure.

At the time, though, everyone was just trying to make it through. They weathered Christmastime blackouts and rationing of gasoline, meat, butter and sugar. They tended to victory gardens and bought war bonds. Some families were uprooted to relocation camps in Arizona. Many coped with the loss of loved ones.

The Star, affected by the rationing of gasoline and tires just like everyone else, was also hampered by censorship. In his 1962 book, "The County Star: My Buena Ventura," Roy Pinkerton recalled regulations preventing the paper from "news coverage of what went on at Port Hueneme, or even mentioning its name," even though thousands of local residents were employed there.

The county's population skyrocketed 11 percent during the war years, and when the war was over, many decided to stay. A Dec. 31, 1945, front page article captured the mood of the time. With the headline, "1946 – When Things Will Be Coming Our Way," the story read, "The new year is the one we've been waiting for – the year when reconversion will be completed and production begins realization of the war years' dream of a new washing machine, a new refrigerator, car, bicycle, camera and what not – including nylons."

That only scratched the surface. In 1948, new construction in the county exceeded $1 million a month.

Left: *Seabees parade in Ventura during a World War II bond rally.* #11594

Right: *American Red Cross, Ojai chapter, during World War II. Peggy Hardy is in the middle of the photograph, and Ruby Peirano is kneeling at right.* #14968

Above: Seabees pause for refreshments during a bond drive. #11599

Left: The Seabee band entertains the crowd during a bond rally. #11601

Above: Marching in step at the junior college field, today's Larrabee Stadium, in 1943. #664

Right: Seabee equipment passes Main and Palm streets in Ventura during a bond rally. #11593

National fundraisers: To raise money for the war, the United States held seven major war loan drives to persuade residents to buy war bonds. War finance committees assigned quotas to counties, which, in turn, assigned quotas to cities. Tallies were printed nearly every day on the front page of The Star. Ventura County's fourth drive, for example went "over the top" on Feb. 8, 1944, exceeding its quota of $4,975,000. Ventura had the largest quota, at $1,592,000, followed by Oxnard-Port Hueneme, Santa Paula, Fillmore, Ojai, Camarillo, Saticoy, Moorpark-Santa Susana and Conejo at $50,000. Among the fundraisers were performances by Rudy Vallee and rides down California Street in military equipment. Admission was the purchase of a war bond.

Right: The Seabee band in action during a war bond drive. #11607

Above: Seabees sing during a bond drive. #11605

Left: Seabees perform during a bond rally. #11604

Above: Pictured left to right are Takeo Susuki, Leonard K. Takasugi and Hisao Matsumoto. Susuki and Takasugi volunteered for the 442nd Regimental Combat Team, the Army unit composed up of Japanese-Americans. It will always remain an odd footnote in U.S. history that while many Americans of Japanese descent were living in relocation camps, the 442nd would become the most decorated unit for its size and length of service in battle in U.S. military history. #28961

Left: Port Hueneme during World War II. #11492

Ventura County: Growing a County

Left: *Relocation camps took some county residents of Japanese descent; the military took others. Here, Leonard Takasugi, on leave from the U.S. Army, visits family member Abe Takasugi who was with his parents at the relocation center at the Gila River Indian Reservation in Arizona. Leonard would later be killed in action in Italy. "It must have been such an ironic situation to see Leonard come back to visit his parents after basic training," cousin Nao Takasugi recalled in a June 18, 1999, Star article. "He had come to say goodbye as he was off to fight for his country. He was in uniform and had come into a barbed wire compound, with armed guards wearing the same uniform he wore. The same government he was fighting for was keeping his family behind the barbed wire."* #27582

Right: *Before World War II, Takeo Susuki was just another kid in Ventura County who loved baseball. Known as Chick, he is shown here in 1939 pitching for Dutch Boys Bread on the Ventura night league team.* #28960

Above: *Takeo Susuki helped lead this team to the Western Division championship in 1939. Shown in the back row are, from left, Billy Campion, Jack Wilson, Frank Wilson, Leroy Williams, Eddie Bernstein, Harley Smith, Tom Donnelly and Bill Kaiser. Among the other players are John Basano, Dalton Clement, Marion Amescua, Larry Chapman, coach Morris "Red" Badgro, manager Art Lovatt, Richard Chapman, Bill Donnelly, Takeo Susuki and Gene Thrift.* #28971

Right: *With baseball a distant memory, 1st Sgt. Takeo Susuki poses outside Camp Shelby, Miss., during World War II.* #28968

Right: Tomio Yeto in the doorway of his store in Saticoy, 1946. #28485

Below: Tomio and Utako Yeto in the Yeto Market, Saticoy, 1930. Their son, John, who was relocated with his family to Tulare, then to Gila River, Ariz., when he was 7 years old, runs the market today. "Before we left for the center, we leased the store to Mrs. Gonzales, and she ran it until we came back in 1945," John recalls. His grandfather had come to the United States from Japan; his father was born in Oxnard in 1907 and worked in the packinghouses, saving his money to buy the market. The Yeto Market moved to its current location, just a few blocks down from the original, in 1971. #28484

Above: Manuel Inadomi with a produce buyer in front of his store in Oxnard, 1932. #28429

Handing Over the Keys:

The Takasugis, the Yetos and the Inadomis all owned markets in Ventura County and were relocated, first to Tulare, then to Gila River in Arizona. The Takasugis, owners of the Asahi Market in Oxnard, "were lucky," recalled a Dec. 2, 1973, Star story. "They rented their business to a Mexican family that successfully managed it during the war. Not everyone was that lucky. Many Japanese lost their life savings, their property and their business when the war started." The family resumed operation of the store, and son Nao, who inherited the market from his father, went on to become a member of the state Assembly. The Yetos also leased their Saticoy store to another family and returned; the Inadomis opened a chain of supermarkets in Southern California.

Above: A panoramic view of Arizona's Gila River relocation center in 1943. "Boy, it was hot," John Yeto recalls. #28225

Right: Internees from the Gila River relocation center pick crops at nearby farms. "It was amazing to see what some of the older Japanese could do with that land," Nao Takasugi recalled in the 1973 Star profile. "It was barren desert, and they got some water from a nearby Indian reservation and made it the most fertile land you've ever seen." #27431

'Everyone Has to Go': In a 1991 oral history on file at the Museum of Ventura County, Teno Kenmotsu Takasugi remembered what it was like when her family was uprooted. "After the war started and they began talking about sending us to camp, our friends in Ventura said that there was no reason to send the Takasugis to camp. The people at the church told us that they weren't picking on us personally but that everyone has to go and no one can stay behind." Mrs. Takasugi died in 1997 at the age of 99. Sons Leonard, Knox and Thomas preceded her in death; they, along with her son George, all served in Europe during World War II while their parents and other siblings remained at Gila River.

Left: A portrait of Ruby Bounds, circa 1931. #14313

Right: Ruby Bounds Peirano in her American Red Cross uniform, at the Ojai chapter, during World War II. #14969

Women in the work force:

Even before Pearl Harbor, women were being recruited for defense efforts. The June 27, 1941, Star reported that 80 county women had signed up for a local unit of the Women's Ambulance and Defense Corps, with weekly drills planned. By Dec. 30, 1944, the number of female recruits for the war effort was huge. A full-page ad in The Star for the Women's Army Corps said 22,000 WACs were needed "at once" to serve as medical technicians in U.S. Army hospitals.

Above: A wooden training boat, Port Hueneme, 1944. #11619

Right: A Red Cross service unit, 1943. #652

Left: Buildings under construction at the Advance Base Depot, Port Hueneme, 1944. #26752

Opposite: The Advance Base Depot at Port Hueneme, circa 1944. In the early days of World War II, Hueneme was used to train Seabees, the Construction Battalion crew. On May 18, 1942, the Hueneme site was officially established as the Advance Base Depot. In 1945, it was renamed the Naval Construction Battalion Center. #26746

Above: Looking north from Hueneme at the former Navy Radio Compass Station. The land behind the buildings is now the naval station. #26365

Right: In 1940, Cal-Aero Corp. opened the Mira Loma Flight Academy at Oxnard Airport for training Army Air Corps cadets. On June 29, 11 Army training planes and 86 student pilots arrived to begin training. The circular layout of the barracks and administration buildings was unusual, according to M.L. Shettle Jr., author of "U.S. Naval Air Stations of World War II." The academy closed June 28, 1944. #26225

Left: *Men moving boxes at Port Hueneme, circa 1944.* #26757

Right: *Small boats are cradled on the dock at the U.S. Naval Advance Base Depot, Port Hueneme, circa 1944.* #26771

Below: *U.S. Naval Advance Base Depot, Port Hueneme, circa 1944. Northwest mechanical crane in operation.* #26750

Above: Seabee equipment on the docks, circa 1944. #26756

"Fighting Seabees:"
Star readers finally learned some details of Port Hueneme's Advance Base Depot and Seabee receiving barracks on March 13, 1944, two years after the Navy took over the area. Reporters from Ventura County and Los Angeles newspapers were taken on an all-day tour of the base under the agreement that the stories run on the same day in the five newspapers represented. Waxed The Star, "We who knew it two years ago as a lazy little commercial port catering to the occasional lumber ships or livestock barges, and had since gazed at it from outside the tightly guarded walls with a reporter's natural lust, were frankly amazed at the sprawling city of more than 20,000 population which has grown up within the confines of Ventura county in 24 short wartime months." The reporters went through live grenade fire and watched the Seabees at target practice – "amazing accuracy for a group of men who are supposed to be builders, not fighters."

Ventura County: Growing a County

Left: U.S. Naval Advance Base Depot, Port Hueneme, circa 1944. #26748

Above: Mechanical equipment being used dockside. #11642

Right: Workers at the Advance Base Depot, Port Hueneme, 1944. #26762

Above: Warehouse storage facility. #11636

Above: A local beach is used as a training ground. Nearly a decade before World War II, the military began using Ventura's beaches and Seaside Park as staging areas for training exercises. "Artillery Unit Will Camp Here For Two Weeks," announced a June 8, 1934, headline. More than 400 men took part that year. The event was successful. "'We'll Be Back!' Says Guard Chief," read an Aug. 16, 1934, headline. #10076

Left: Row of trucks at the Advance Base Depot, circa 1944. #26781

"Strategic Location":
As early as 1935, the military recognized Ventura County's importance to national security. "County Is Strategic Defense Location," read an Oct. 28, 1935, headline above an interview with an anti-aircraft division instructor who called the county "one of the most strategical points in Southern California." "We are sure that invaders would try to land in that section and attempt to march up the Santa Clara river in an effort to reach the railroad running into the San Joaquin valley and also to cut off power, water and communication lines to Los Angeles," the officer said. "Also, the coast railroad goes through your district, which would be an objective of invaders."

The Manpower Shortage: With men at war, women were called into duty. A March 8, 1943, Star article carrying the headline "More County Women Must Get Into War Effort" urged women to do their part. "More Ventura county women will have to forego bridge parties and daytime social affairs if this area is to keep up with its needs for workers," the story read. Roy Pinkerton of The Star wrote in his book that women saved his publication. "Our men employees left in a steady stream for the armed forces," Pinkerton wrote. "For replacements, we had to depend on a man with a 4-F draft classification or, nine times out of ten, on women. The women, with what training we surviving males could hurriedly import, were wonderful. God bless the World War II women!"

Left: Men working dockside at Port Hueneme. #11649

Opposite: Women went to work in World War II, the age of Rosie the Riveter. Here, three women type at the Advance Base Depot, circa 1944. #26778

Above: Swimming pools at Port Hueneme. #11629

Right: A woman works at a typewriting-bookkeeping machine at the Advance Base Depot, circa 1944. #26765

POW Camp: Ventura County was home to one prisoner-of-war camp, an establishment near today's Rio Mesa High School that held Germans. The Star ran a story on Nov. 26, 1996, interviewing Jeffrey Geiger, who had researched the camp for a book, and Saticoy residents who had brought in remnants of the camp, including woodcarvings crafted by some of the prisoners. According to Geiger, the camp covered about 18 acres and was designed to hold 500 prisoners. While the Army provided guards and equipment, such as cots and dishes, it was local ranchers who put together the $100,000 for the camp to be built. Why? Prisoners at Camp Cooke, where Vandenberg Air Force Base is today, were used to harvest local crops, and Venturans were eager to have the same labor force. The camp was in place from May 1945 until spring 1946.

Right: Seabees in a bus loading area. #11645

Above: Seabees at work at drafting tables, Port Hueneme. #11615

Left: Seabees in formation on the depot parade grounds. #11637

Above: *Ojai Valley Inn's golf course was converted to a camp for Company C-1 during wartime.* #28083

Above: *A pile driver in the dock area of Port Hueneme.* #26759

Left: *A Navy band strikes up a tune.* #11644

Left: Military men look toward port as their ship makes its way toward the docks. #17195

Right: 1st Lt. Edwin Pinkerton perches on the wing of his Mustang fighter pilot in 1944. A Santa Paula native, Pinkerton died in August 1944 when he was shot down over France, having completed more than 32 missions. #10009

Above: Carl A. Brown poses by his military aircraft. Brown called these planes the "ships" that gave the enemy a bad time in Burma. #17194

Left: Carl A. Brown in his World War II military uniform, 1945. #17191

Above: Carpenters work at the Advance Base Depot. #11647

The Future: "Post-War Planning Group Organization Under Way," read the Feb. 29, 1944, Star headline. Some 75 business and civic leaders had already begun drawing up plans to deal with distribution of war surpluses, disposal of government-owned war plants, paying for conversion of industry and relocation of manpower. One of the biggest postwar changes for Ventura County was the establishment of the $30 million Point Mugu Naval Air Missile Test Center. Among those touring it on New Year's Eve, 1949, was a young congressman, Richard M. Nixon.

Above: Ventura County reaped postwar riches. Here, Oak View volunteer firefighters pose in front of a firetruck that was war surplus material. #19007

Above: Port Hueneme Officers' Club in Bard Mansion, 1946. #10509

Left: NROTC Cadet Wyman Spalding on the USS Oscar Badger. #27673

Right: A group assembled in front of the Contractors Pacific Naval Air Bases Payroll Office. #26772

Ventura County: Growing a County

Enjoying Life

Between the stresses of the Depression and the anxiety brought on by World War II, Ventura County needed a chance to let loose – and it did a great job of that.

Baseball, football, softball and basketball teams thrived. Horse races were a big draw at Seaside Park, as were the Portland Beavers, a Pacific Coast League baseball club that held spring training there during the 1930s. In March 1934, the Beavers played the Chicago Cubs in an exhibition game to what the March 20 Star called an "overflow throng." Alas, the Cubs won, 7 to 3.

The Ojai Tennis Tournament continued its long tradition, and golf, boxing and ocean sports such as fishing and sailing remained popular.

Meanwhile, Ventura County residents continued their search for something to replace the County Fair, which took a 10-year hiatus in the 1930s due to lack of funding. The Days of the Golden West fit the bill. For several years beginning in 1933, thousands of people would come to Ventura for a spring celebration that included a parade, a stampede and a Western show.

And in 1930, another Ventura tradition began. "Monster 'V' Put On Hill; Buccaneers Inscribe Whitewash Letter On City Height," read the Feb. 14 headline. Students at what was then called Ventura Union High School had painted the 150-foot letter overnight.

Left: *The Ventura County Braves baseball team, 1950.* #17971

Right: *Men on horseback race in Ojai.* #10423

Ventura County: Growing a County

Above: Ventura Police Boys Club baseball team at Babe Ruth Field in Seaside Park, 1949. Ruth came to Ventura in 1931 to visit Gus Gleichman, proprietor of the Pierpont Inn and a former Baltimore Oriole. Ruth began his professional career with the Orioles. "Babe Talks Old Times," read the Oct. 30 headline. #18816

Left: The Ventura Yankees, a farm team operated by the New York Yankees, 1947. In uniform are, back row from left: Don Murray, Len Noren, Bob Webster, Doug Essick, Art Dyck, Dick Morgan, Ted Bell, Arnie Lambeck and Archie Wilson. Middle row, from left: Charlie Noah, Gil Hawkins, Gene Valla, Ralph Sanhammer, Johnny Sturman, Frank Ciremeli, Tony Klesira, Lyman Stone and Bill Hyland. #29643

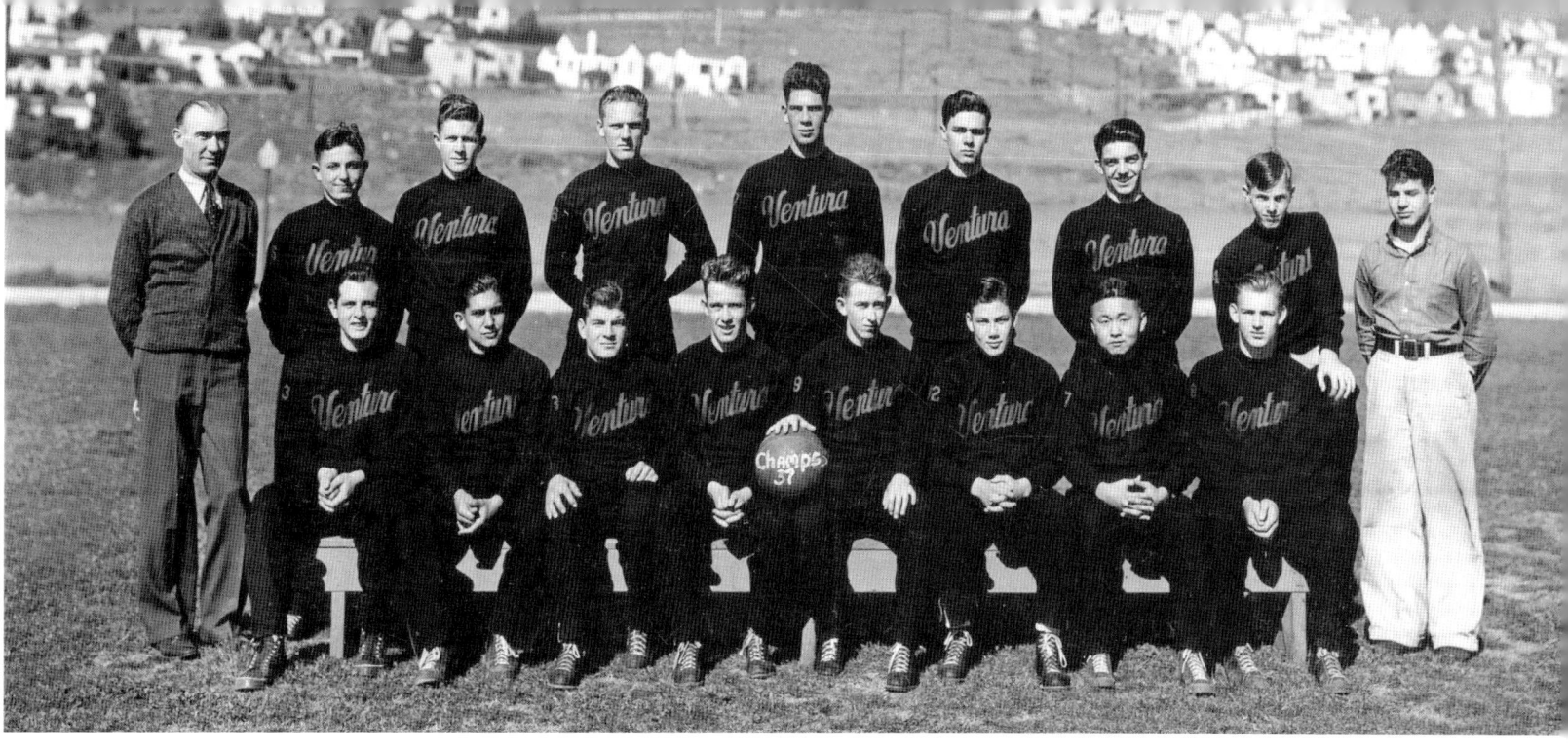

Right: Ventura High School basketball team champions, Ventura County League, 1937. Standing, from left, are Coach Joe Buckmaster, Larry Chapman, Warren Taylor, Bob Stroble, Ellsworth Suytar, Allen Petit, Joe Pierano, Keith Clark and Manager Art K. Lovatt Jr. Sitting, from left, are Ronald Byron, Jim Bentley, Jim Deering, William Donnelly, Captain Thomas Donnelly, Marion Amescua, Takeo Susuki and Don MacIssac. #28970

Above: The Police Boys Club softball team, 1948. #18817

Left: Dutch Boys Bread team, the Ventura night league champions. Standing, from left, are Dick Coffey, Joe Lorenzana, Jack Wigton, Huren Rololand, Junior Suytar, Phil Marquez and William Schumacher. Kneeling, from left, are Takeo Susuki, Harley Smith, Chick Peters, Lolo Gonzales, Eddie Griego and Frank Wilson. #28972

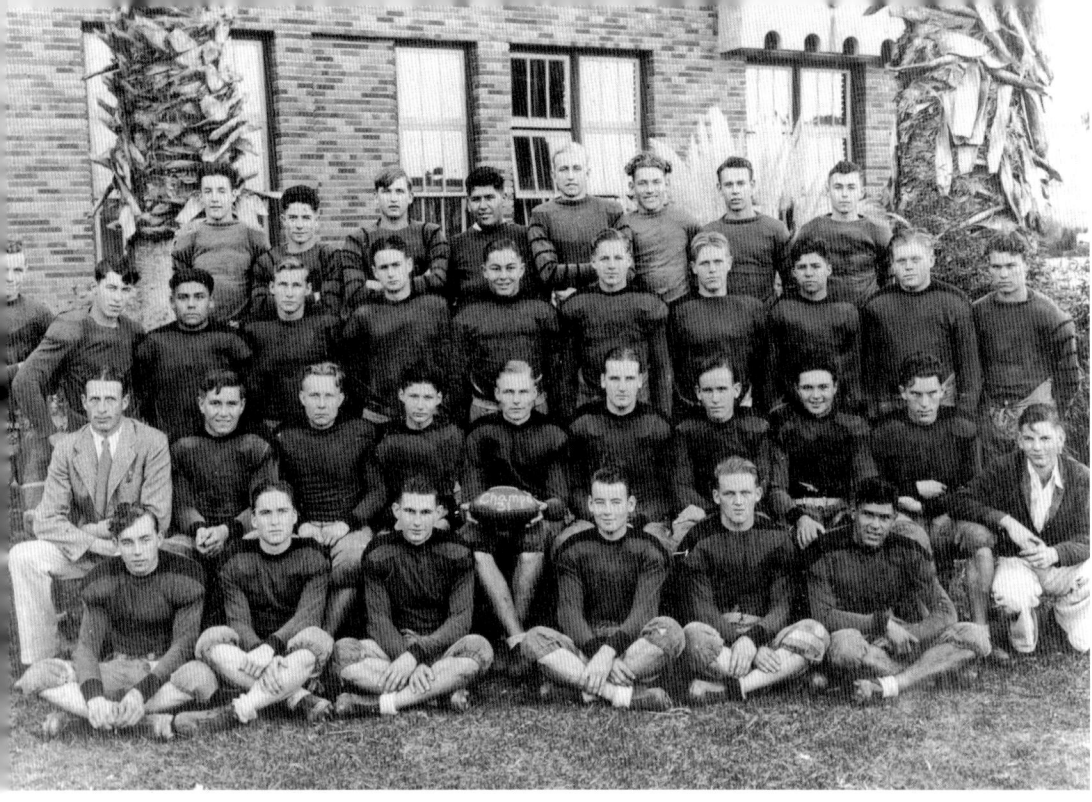

Above: The Ojai Valley Tennis Tournament at Libbey Park, a longstanding tradition in Ventura County. #10404

Above: The 1931 Ventura High School champion football team, coached by Eric Kolberg. "Pirates Defeat Fillmore to Win," read the Dec. 7 headline. "Ventura Squad On Long End Of 18-to-0 Score; Successful Season For Local Boys Comes To End." Pictured are, back row from left, Gail Gordon, Ray Faulk, Jack Borrell, Ray Garcia, Mr. Sandoz, R. Grant, Marion M. Grant, and Mr. Bowker. Third row from left are Harold Mears, Dean Crow, Ray Montoya, Norman Gallagher, Mr. Duffy, Rawland Freear, Ray Armstrong, Dan Van Dellen, Edward Vanegas, Deerheart Neilson and Jack Withers. Second row from left are Coach Eric Kolberg, Edward Hickerson, Mr. Bruce, Richard Deck, Captain Bob Steele, Richard Carlin, Clyde Woolley, Charles Hall, Carl Neal and Manager Don Lang. Front row from left are Ray Lamp, Paul Berg, Hugh Garman, Bob Sorem, Bill Dysart and William Flores. #17762

Right: Golf course, circa 1935. #18669

128 Enjoying Life

Left: This photo, taken in 1932, is of Leroy Gibson, Sr., who was known as the "Wichita Wildcat" in professional boxing. Gibson was a resident of Ventura and founder of Gibson Barbecue on Figueroa Street. #25532

Above: World famous boxer Joe Louis visits Oxnard in 1946. This photo was taken in front of the Carnegie Library. Johnson's Radio Service car was used to amplify sound. #14115

Left: Boxing match between two 9-year-old boys at a 1948 holiday party held at the Police Boys Club House. #10349

Left: *Harness racing, part of the action at the Ventura County Fairgrounds racetrack, circa 1940. By 1934, Ventura had become a popular racing venue. "47 Race Horses Headquartered In Seaside Park," read a Sept. 14, 1934, headline above an article stating that the park was "rapidly developing as an important factor in the racing game of the state." The industry was pumping an estimated $4,000 a month into the city's economy, primarily via leather shops, drug and hardware stores, farriers, restaurants and hotels.* #2635

Above: *Ventura County Fairgrounds racetrack, circa 1940.* #26354

Right: *Ventura, looking east from beyond the Ventura River. Seaside Park hosted everything from horse races to kite-flying contests, from military drills to movie shoots.* #7605

Above: Fourth Annual Older Girls Conference of Southern California, April 30, 1939, held in Ventura. The photo was taken outside the bathhouse at the foot of California Street. #7179

Left: For those who could afford a boat, sailing was a popular pastime. Here, Don Louie Robertson is shown at Point Mugu, circa 1930. His cabin can be seen in the background. #10117

Right: Dr. J.C. Vorbeck enjoys a longtime ocean sport on Ventura Beach in 1946. #28744

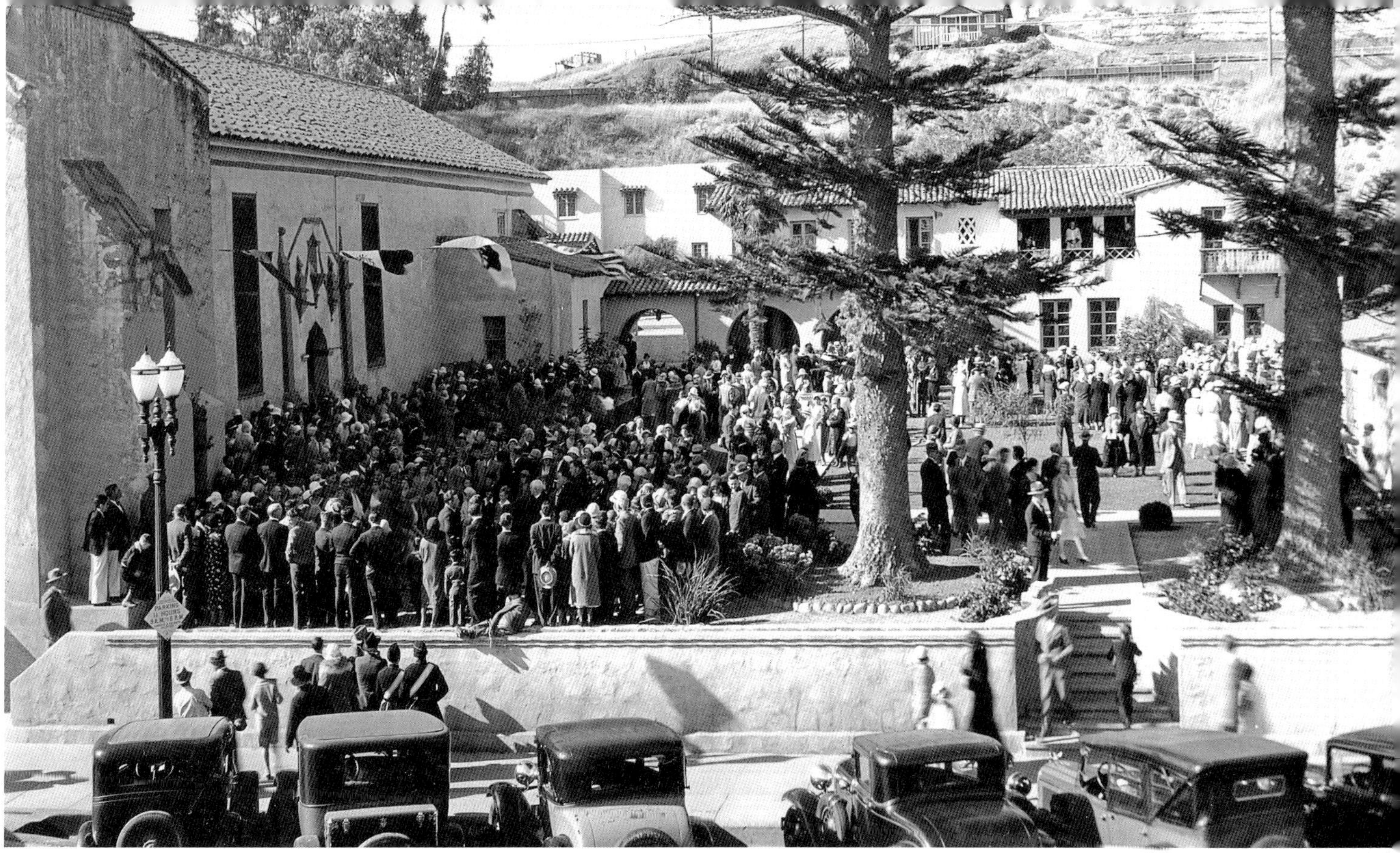

Above: *The San Buenaventura Mission sesquicentennial and tree-planting ceremony celebrating the 150th anniversary of the mission, April 3, 1932.* #7660

Left: *Days of the Golden West group, outside Ventura County Courthouse, 1934.* #5202

Right: *San Buenaventura Mission sesquicentennial celebration, April 3, 1932.* #7627

Above: Somis-Camarillo 4-H Club members on a decorated float for a Ventura street fair, circa 1930s. #15236

Above: The 150th anniversary of the mission is celebrated with a re-enactment at the Father Serra Cross, 1932. The cross above Ventura would have many adventures. It was toppled by heavy winds in February 1941. And in 1937, a creative Depression-era gentleman figured out how to tap less-than-spiritual power from the structure. "Home Lighted From Cross," read the April 29 headline. "Trailer Resident, From Santa Barbara, Takes Electricity From Father Serra Cross." The man had tapped the electricity used to light the cross and had "rerouted the juice to his trailer," the story reported. He was discovered by local residents curious about the odd lights near the cross. Edison declined to prosecute; the man was released with a warning. #1094

Right: Ventura Police Boys Club marching unit standing at present arms, just prior to marching in the 1948 Ventura County Parade. #10347

Enjoying Life

The Rose Parade: For many years, Ventura entered a float in Pasadena's Tournament of Roses parade. In January 1934, Ventura took second prize in its division of cities under 20,000. Catalina Island came in first. The float, an enormous lobster, cost $300 to build and was put on display at Ventura Junior College.

The parade that year was plagued with trouble. "Los Angeles Area Suffers Worst Storm In History," read the Jan. 2, 1934, headline. Forty-two Southern Californians died in the storm. The weather delayed the Ventura Junior College Band, which was supposed to march in the parade. The band arrived at the last minute and fell in line at the end of the parade, but because they were late, band members were denied entrance to the football game at the Rose Bowl. The game ended up being a major upset, with Columbia defeating the heavily favored Stanford 7 to 0. After receiving a scathing letter from Venturans, Tournament of Roses officials apologized.

Above: A wagon makes its way down Main Street during a 1933 parade. #25129

Left: The mission's sesquicentennial is celebrated at Grant Park above Ventura, 1932. #9170

Below: Chow line for Ventura County Boys Club members after winning first place for marching in the 1948 Ventura County Fair Parade. #10348

Above: Portuguese Crown Club Queen Virginia Faria, center, and attendant Sadi Silva, left, on the steps of Santa Clara Church in Oxnard, 1930. #27057

Left: The Queen Parade at Portuguese Crown Hall, June 1937. Pictured are Queen Evelyn Silva, maids Dorothy Corella and Evelyn Dominguez. Cape holders are Frank Silva, Jr. and Cecilio Oliver. Children: Barbara Sousa, Johnnie Silveira, Lavelle Rotsler, and Adeline Avilla. #26990

Below: Parade, May 24, 1935. #2866

Left: A picnic and barbecue at Seaside Park, June 1928. #2689

Above: Pioneer Picnic, 1931. This was an annual event held at Foster Park; the 1936 event drew more than 500 participants. Foster Park was also the site for 1934 reunion of ex-Missourians. "2,500 Former Missourians Stage Picnic," read the June 18, 1934, headline. The picnic was hosted by the Ventura County Missourians Society. #5581

Right: Oxnard Buddhist Church members show two Japanese dignitaries the Point Mugu fish camp in 1931. From left are: Mr. M. Takeda, Mr. Y. Yamashita, Mr. Konamori, Mrs. Kubota, Mr. T. Moriwaki, Mr. Kubota (owner of fish camp), two visitors from Japan, Mr. S. Watarida, Mr. Yeto, Mr. K. Iwamoto, Mr. M. amoto, Mr. S. Inouye, Mr. T. Shiozaki. #27412

Days of the Golden West:

The 1933 Days of the Golden West parade was three miles long and included 25 carloads of 1849 Boosters from Taft and Maricopa who had driven over the Maricopa Highway, a road that was yet to be officially opened. "Brilliant Parade Opens Celebration," read the May 27, 1933, headline. "Thousands Line Streets To See Thousands Parade."

The 1934 event also was a huge success. "Everyone In City Out In Costume For Celebration," roared the May 23, 1934, headline. "Antique Autos and Bathing Beauties Featured," read the May 25 parade headline. And finally, on May 28, "Days Of Golden West Event Has Glorious Close; Estimate 15,000 At Three Sessions Of Big Rodeo; More Than 700 Horses Paraded; Gate Receipts Are Expected To Be About $5,000." In fact, they totaled $6,491.64, just $151.29 short of breaking even.

Not everyone was pleased with the event, however. In early 1935, the San Buenaventura Women's Club objected to the use of tax money for the event. "There has been much talk among not only the women of the club but many other women in the city regarding the manner in which the celebration has been carried on, and especially regarding drunkenness," the club president was quoted as saying in a Feb. 12, 1935, article. "We have learned that many mothers took their children away from the city over the weekend of the celebration last year to keep them out of the undesirable surroundings." The event went on as planned that year.

Above: *A parade down Oxnard's Fifth Street.* #26341

Left: *Days of the Golden West Stampede, Ventura, May 27, 1933.* #10126

Opposite: *Ventura County Courthouse employees in costume during the Days of the Golden West celebration in 1933.* #8367

Ventura County: Growing a County

Above: The 1849 Boosters line up on Maricopa Road on May 15, 1934, on their way to Ventura for the Days of the Golden West celebration. Members from Kern, Ventura, Santa Paula, Oxnard and Bakersfield are represented. #5174

Right: The Santa Paula Band joins the 1849 Boosters in Taft on May 15, 1934. #5182

Below: The 1849 Boosters leave Maricopa on May 15, 1934. #2148

Above: *The Fife, Drum and Bugle Corps from the Ventura Sons and Daughters of American Legion. This photo was taken in spring of 1939 at Seaside Park.* #8747

Left: *1934 Obon Festival Committee and dancers inside First Buddhist Church on Sixth Street, Oxnard.* #27425

Out of Room: Occasionally, events were too big for the city to handle. "Rooms Needed For Visitors At Day Meet," read an April 17, 1937, headline above an article detailing plans for an upcoming state convention of the Disabled American Veterans. "Not Enough Hotels In City For 2,000 At June Conclave."

Viewing Our Past

Aerial photos, impossible until after the turn of the century, offer a whole new perspective of Ventura County. When examined, they show growth dictated by the ocean, the mountains, the oil fields and the farms and ranches.

The following photos are snapshots of growth and change – a peek at the past, a glimpse of the future, an explanation of the present.

Left: *Looking west from the beach in Ventura, 1935.* #7606

Right: *Ojai Arcade, circa 1930.* #26351

Above: Main Street in Ventura, looking west from Fir Street. The speed limit signs painted in the middle of the street were a staple of World War II-era America. #10334

Left: An aerial view of Ventura from Pierpont Beach looking west, 1936. #10687

Above: View from Cedar Street onto Wall Street in Ventura, May 1933. #10729

Right: Mrs. Clyde Harkness' garden, 944 E. Santa Clara St., Ventura, 1930. #8804

Left: Stagecoach Inn at Newbury Park. At the time this photo was taken, in 1942, the building was at the southwest corner of Ventu Park Road and Highway 101, and it housed a boys military school. Built in 1876 as the Grand Union Hotel, offering luxurious accommodations for those traveling between Los Angeles and Santa Barbara, it would serve as a post office, a tearoom, a restaurant, a gift shop and a museum before burning to the ground in 1970. It was rebuilt at its present location at 51 S. Ventu Park Road and opened as the Stagecoach Inn Museum in 1976. #7387

Above: Main Street looking west toward Seaward Avenue in Ventura. #10336

Left: Chismahoo Ranch, circa 1937. This property west of Oak View was submerged with the creation of Lake Casitas. #14449

Above: The Oxnard Harbor District Office, at Market and Main Streets, circa 1930s. #10627

Right: Ventura City Hall has had many homes through the years. Around 1940, it was on the ground floor of the Masonic Temple. Here, construction begins on its new quarters, circa 1950. Today, city offices are in the old Ventura County Courthouse, and a bank currently occupies the building under construction in this photo. #10377

Above: Port Hueneme shoreline and buildings. #8374

Left: Plaza Park, Oxnard. #26540

Ventura County: Growing a County

Above: Marjorie Norton, in tube, and Gwen Norton enjoy Lyons Pool, circa 1939. The area, known through the years as Cliff Glen or Lyons Springs, was destroyed when Matilija Dam was constructed. #16808

Left: Beulah Strobel, left, Violette Weigle, right, Jackie and Johnny Strobel, middle, at an old swimming hole above Wheeler Hot Springs, 1936. #15055

Right: The lighthouse on Anacapa Island, 1933. #2119

Opposite: A view from Poli Street looking south at night, Ventura, 1939. Oil tankers off shore could load all night with lights. #18638

Above: The north side of Main Street between California and Oak streets, circa 1940. The Hotel Ventura at California and Main streets still exists. #26360

Right: Ventura, 1935. #7538

Above: A street scene at the corner of B and Fifth streets, looking east toward Oxnard Boulevard, circa 1940. #25486

Left: The Moorpark intersection on Highway 118, about 1940. #26638.

Left: *Looking east on Fifth Street across Oxnard Boulevard, Oxnard, April 1947.* #13018

Above: *Looking northeast at Oxnard Boulevard and Third Street, Oxnard, 1947.* #13024

Right: *Aerial view of Fillmore, 1947.* #9684-83

Above: An early view of Oxnard Boulevard. #26596

Left: Main Street in Ojai, 1948, showing the Pergola, the Post Office and a dusting of snow. #10431

Right: The Ojai Valley Inn and Country Club. #10758

Below: Oxnard Boulevard between Sixth and Seventh streets, looking south. #26595

Ventura County: Growing a County

Index

56th Coast Artillery Regiment ... 30
442nd Regimental Combat Team ... 105
1849 Boosters driving to Ventura on Maricopa Highway ... 139

A

Abplanalp, Helen ... 20
Adams, John Quincy ... 8
Advance Base Depot, Port Hueneme
  carpenters at work ... 122
  construction of ... 110
  mechanical cranes ... 113, 114
  reporters tour of ... 113
  Seabees at ... 111, 118
  small boats stored at ... 113
  U.S. Navy trucks ... 115
  warehouse storage facility ... 115
  women working at ... 116–17
  See also Seabees
"After the Sunset" (movie) ... 45
agricultural industry ... 32–37
  apricot harvest, Elliott Hendry Ranch, Moorpark ... 37
  bean planting tractor ... 35
  bean threshing ... 6–7, 7
  beet sugar factory, Oxnard ... 35, 36
  citrus crop ... 32–33, 67
  lemon packing house interior ... 32–33
  lima bean growers barbecue in Seaside Park ... 34
  loading silage into a silo ... 34
  retrospective ... 33
  vegetable harvest ... 34
  See also lima beans
airplanes
  Cal-Aero Corp flight academy for training cadets ... 110
  Curtiss-Wright C-46 crash ... 98
  military aircraft ... 121
  Mustang fighter pilot ... 121
  P-38 crash in upper Tapo Canyon ... 98
  parade exhibit ... 136
  SNJ-type aircraft crash landing site ... 98
airports
  Oxnard Airport ... 27, 110
  Santa Paula Airport ... 26, 27, 89
Al. G. Wilson Dynamometer Service, Ventura ... 64
"All Quiet on the Western Front" (movie) ... 44
American Crystal Sugar Company ... 36
American Federation of Labor ... 47
American Legion Fife, Drum and Bugle Corps at Seaside Park, Ventura ... 141
American Red Cross ... 101, 109
American Sailor (training ship) ... 20
Amescua, Marion ... 106, 127
Anacapa Island lighthouse ... 148
anchovies ... 51
Anderson, Marcella Wilson ... 64
Anderson 8 oil well ... 30
Anderson 19 oil well ... 30
Andrade, Joe ... 58
apricot harvest, Elliott Hendry Ranch, Moorpark ... 37
Arizona, Gila River Indian Reservation relocation center ... 106–8
Armstrong, Ray ... 128
Army Air Corps cadets training in Oxnard ... 110
art critics on Gordon grant's mural in Ventura Post Office ... 13
Arya Vihara estate near Ojai ... 75
Asahi Market, Oxnard ... 107
Associated Oil Company
  fishermen on launch of ... 11
  lunch wrecked by December 1935 high seas ... 99
automobiles and trucks
  1901 Cadillac ... 64
  1941 Pontiac advertisement ... 68
  Bill Baker's Bakery delivery fleet ... 49
  carloads of 1849 Boosters driving to Ventura on Maricopa Highway ... 139, 140
  Coca-Cola delivery trucks ... 59
  Hobson Bros. Packing Company refrigerated truck ... 55, 69
  Johnson's Radio Service sound car ... 129
  Ojai Good Bread delivery trucks ... 51
  at Pierpont Bay ... 48
  repair services ... 58, 64, 68
  tow truck at Joe Andrade's Garage ... 58
  U.S. Navy trucks at Advance Base Depot, Port Hueneme ... 115
  at Ventura Pipe & Construction Co. ... 55
the Avenue oil field
  production numbers ... 29
  security measures during WWII ... 30
  and Ventura River flooding ... 91, 92
Avilla, Adeline ... 136

B

Babe Ruth Field in Seaside Park, Ventura ... 126
Badgro, Morris "Red" ... 106
Baker, Bill ... 49, 50
Balcom Canyon Road as work relief project ... 7
B and Fifth Streets, Oxnard ... 150
Bard, Thomas ... 15
Bard Mansion, Port Hueneme ... 123
Bard Sanitarium, Ventura ... 77
Bardsdale, snowfall in ... 85
Basano, John ... 106
baseball teams
  Dutch Boys Bread ... 106, 127
  Ventura County Braves ... 124–25
  Ventura Police Boys Club ... 126
  Ventura Yankees ... 126
basketball team, Ventura County League 1937 champions ... 127
Bear Canyon fire ... 92
beet sugar factory, Oxnard ... 35, 36
Bell, Ted ... 126
Bentley, Jim ... 127
Berg, Paul ... 128
Bernstein, Eddie ... 106
Bill Baker's Bakery, Ojai ... 49, 50, 51
bond rallies in Ventura County ... 100–103
Borrell, Jack ... 128
Bounds, Ruby ... 109
Bowker, Mr. ... 128
boxing
  Joe Lewis visits Oxnard ... 129
  match between 9-year-olds ... 129
  "Wichita Wildcat" of Ventura ... 129
Boys Club, Ojai ... 83
Boy Scout meeting, regional ... 81
Brosnan, Pierce ... 45
Brown, Carl A. ... 121
Brown, Joe E. ... 50
Bruce, Mr. ... 128
Buckmaster, Joe ... 127
Buddhist Church of Oxnard ... 75, 137
Buenaventura Women's Club objections to Days of the Golden West celebration ... 139
building. *See* construction industry
Byron, Ronald ... 127

C

cake from Bill Baker's Bakery ... 50
Cal-Aero Corporation ... 110
California and Main Streets flooded, Ventura ... 96
California Department of Parks and Recreation ... 30
California Highway Patrol ... 72
California National Guard ... 30
Calleguas Creek Bridge construction ... 27
Camarillo Heights, looking south from ... 33
Camarillo Mercantile ... 66
Camarillo State Hospital ... 77, 81
camel from Goebel's Lion Farm ... 41
Camp Edna Girl Scout Camp, Matilija Lake ... 76
Campion, Billy ... 106
Camp Shelby, Miss. ... 106
Carlin, Richard ... 128
Carnegie Library, Oxnard ... 129
Carr, Tom ... 81
cars. *See* automobiles and trucks
Casa de Rosas Club ... 77
Cedar fire in San Diego County ... 93
Chaffee, Walter ... 86
Chancelor–Canfield–Midway Oil ... 29
Chapman, Larry ... 106, 127
Chapman, Richard ... 106
Chismahoo Ranch, west of Oak View ... 146
Chumas basket with lightning design ... 4
churches. *See* religions
Ciremeli, Frank ... 126
citrus crop ... 33, 67
Clark, Keith ... 127
Clark, Tom ... 19
Clement, Dalton ... 106
Coca-Cola Bottling Company, Ventura ... 59
Coca-Cola delivery trucks ... 59

Coffey, Dick 127
Coleman, Meg 20
community. *See* enjoyment and relaxation; public services
Conejo Pass, completion of 16
Conejo Valley, Russell Ranch 44
Congregational Church, Ventura 74
construction industry 14–27
Calleguas Creek Bridge 27
Conejo Pass completion 16
demolishing old hotels 53
Highway 1 19, 20
and labor unions 47
Maricopa Highway 16–19
post-WWII boom 101
rebuilding Foothills Hotel 54
rebuilding Ventura Theater at Chestnut and Main 53
Ventura Pipe and Construction Company 55
and work relief projects 7, 8, 81
Contractors Pacific Naval Air Bases Payroll Office 123
Cooper, Gary 39, 40
Coos Bay, hull of 98
Corella, Dorothy 136
Corriganville 39
"The County Star: My Buena Ventura" (Pinkerton) 101
Crane, Mr. and Mrs. 34
Crawford, Broderick 39
Crow, Dean 128
"The Crowd Roars" (movie) 39
Cruise, Tom 45
Cryctal Brand Sugar, Oxnard 36
Cuban sharks off Ventura wharf 11
Curtiss-Wright C-46 crash 98
Cuyama Valley from Maricopa Highway 17

D

Days of the Golden West celebration, Ventura
1849 Boosters driving to Ventura on Maricopa Highway 139, 140
group dressed up for 138
parade 139
as replacement for County Fair 125
scenery on the way 18, 19
stampede 139
Deck, Richard 128
Deering, Jim 127
DeLeon Hotel destruction, Ventura 53
Delta Theta Tau Sorority installation, Pierpont Inn 81
the Depression. *See* Great Depression
Dillinger, John 71
Disabled American Veterans Convention hotel room shortage 141
disasters 84–99
airplane crashes 98
earthquake 85
floods 85, 96
from heavy seas 85, 94, 95, 97, 98
retrospective 85
See also fires; March 1938 storms and floods; weather
Dojo Sukui dance at Buddhist Church of Oxnard 75
Dominguez, Evelyn 136
Donnelly, Bill 106
Donnelly, Thomas 127
Donnelly, Tom 106
Donnelly, William 127
Duffy, Mr. 128
Dutch Boys Bread baseball team 106, 127
Dyck, Art 126
Dysart, Bill 128

E

earthquake 85
economic growth 46–69
area businesses 58–61, 66–68
auto repair services 58, 64, 68
Bill Baker's Bakery, Ojai 49, 50, 51
cars lined up at Ventura Pipe & Construction Co. 55
fishing industry 51, 52
Hobson Bros. Packing Co. refrigerated truck 55, 69
and labor unions 47
Oxnard Canners, Port Hueneme 53
Pacific Telephone, Ventura 63
Peoples Lumber Company 63
at Pierpont Bay 48
post-WWII expansion 5
retrospective 47
See also construction industry; enjoyment and relaxation; oil industry
1849 Boosters driving to Ventura on Maricopa Highway 140
elephants from Goebel's Lion Farm 40
Elliott Hendry Ranch apricot harvest, Moorpark 37
Ellwood oil field north of Santa Barbara 30
Emma Wood State Beach 30
enjoyment and relaxation 124–41
American Legion Fife, Drum and Bugle Corps at Seaside Park, Ventura 141
boxing 129
Boys Club, Ojai 83
Dutch Boys Bread baseball team 106, 127
ex-Missourians reunion in Foster Park 137
fishing 10, 11, 131
4-H Club members on float for Ventura street fair 134
Girl Scout Camps 76, 78
golfing 128
harness racing, Ventura County Fairgrounds 130
horse race in Ojai 125
Ojai Valley Tennis Tournament at Libbey Park 125, 128
Pasadena Tournament of Roses parade float, Ventura 135
Queen Parade at Portuguese Crown Hall 136
retrospective 125
sailing 131
sunbathers and swimmers at the beach 48
Sunday beach crowd at Hueneme 46–47
Ventura County Boys Club 135
Ventura County Braves baseball team 124–25
Ventura High School 1931 champion football team 128
Ventura High School basketball team 127
Ventura Police Boys Club 126, 127, 129, 134
Ventura Yankees baseball team 126
women stretching on the beach in Oxnard 47
See also Days of the Golden West celebration; public services
Esaki, Roy 61
"Esquadrille" (movie) 45
Essick, Doug 126
ex-Missourians reunion in Foster Park 137

F

Faria, Virginia 136
Farm Security Administration importation of Mexicans 33
Father Junipero Serra statute 8, 13
Father Serra Cross reenactment 134
Faulk, Ray 128
"A Few Good Men" (movie) 45
Fife, Drum and Bugle Corps of the Ventura Sons and Daughters of the American Legion at Seaside Park, Ventura 141
Fillmore
aerial view 34, 151
March 1938 storms washout bridge between Santa Paula and 88
snowfall in 85
washed-out highway and railroad west of 89
fire departments
fire station groundbreaking 81
Oak View volunteer firefighters 123
Ojai Fire Station as work relief project 8
Santa Paula Fire Station as work relief project 7
fires
Bear Canyon fire 92
Cedar fire in San Diego County 93
Goebels Lion Farm 41
Matilija fire 93
McFarland Drive and Ventura Avenue fire 98
Ojai-Maricopa fire 93
Peoples Lumber Company 63
Senõr Canyon (now Senior Canyon) backfire during Ojai-Maricopa Fire 93
Ventura Wharf and Warehouse Company pier fire 84–85, 86
Zaca fire in Santa Barbara and Ventura Counties 93
fire station groundbreaking 81
First Baptist Church, Ventura 74
fish camp at Point Mugu 95
fishing 10, 11
fishing boats at Port Hueneme 52
fishing industry
anchovies at Point Mugu 51
economic growth of 51, 52
fish camp at Point Mugu 95
Hueneme Fisheries Company fishing dock, Port Hueneme 52
Papa Shima mending nets for anchovy fishing 51
FJ-3 Furies aircraft 5
floods
California and Main Streets, Ventura 96
Ventura River flood of 1905 compared to March 1938 storms 85
See also March 1938 storms
Flores, Cuco 57
Flores, William 128
football, Ventura High School 1931 champion team 128
Foothills Hotel, original and rebuilt, Ojai 54
Foster Park 137
4-H Club members on float for Ventura street fair 134
Freear, Rawland 128

G

Gable, Clark 39
Gallagher, Norman 128
Garcia, Ray 128
Garman, Hugh 128
General Machine Company, Ventura 98
George Stuart Historical Figures® 4
Gibson, Hope 83

Ventura County: Growing a County 155

Gibson, Leroy, Sr. "Wichita Wildcat" 129
Gibson, Ruth 78
Gila River Indian Reservation relocation center, Arizona 106–8
Girl Scout Camp
    at Lake Glenn 78
    at Matilija Lake 76
Gleichman, Gus 126
Goebel, Kathy 40, 41
Goebel, Louis 41
Goebel's Lion Farm, Thousand Oaks 39, 40, 41
golfing 128
Gonzales, Lolo 127
Gonzales, Mrs. 107
Gordon, Gail 128
Granger, Stewart 45
Grant, Gordon 13
Grant, Marion M. 128
Grant, R. 128
Grant Park, Ventura 135
Great Depression 6–13
    and agriculture 34
    effect of 5
    and fishing 10–11
    retrospective 7
    Ventura County Fair, 1930 vs. 1940 attendance 9
    waning of 47
    work relief projects 7, 8, 13, 81
Greyhound representative 59
Griego, Eddie 127
Grimm, Mary 20

H

halibut fishing off local pier 11
Hall, Charles 128
Hall, Fred 67
Hardy, Peggy 101
Harkness, Mrs. Clyde, garden of, Ventura 144
harness racing, Ventura County Fairgrounds 130
harvest. *See* agricultural industry
Hawkins, Gil 126
Hayak, Salma 45
health care and health care facilities
    Bard Sanitarium 77
    Camarillo State Hospital 77, 81
    Santa Paula Hospital 77
    Ventura County Hospital 77
Heard, Mrs. Bartlett B. 82
heavy seas 85, 94, 95, 97, 98
Hickerson, Edward 128
"High, Wide and Handsome" (movie) 41
Highway 1
    construction of 19
    opening of Coast Road from Oxnard 19
    sea wall at Point Mugu 20
Highway 118 at Moorpark intersection 150
highway billboards, ban of 19
highway to Santa Barbara one mile west of Ventura 5
Hobson Bros. Packing Company refrigerated truck 55, 69
Hollywood by-the-sea, Oxnard 45
Hopkins, Miriam 45
Hotel Anacapa, Ventura 13
Hotel Ventura, Ventura 150
Hovley, Meg Coleman 20
Howry, Joe R. 5

The Hub, Ojai 66
Hueneme
    fishing on the beach near 10
    Hueneme Wharf and Warehouse Company 52
    pier washed out and rebuilt years later 95
    Point Hueneme Lighthouse 22, 23, 24, 25
    recreation center 35
    Sunday beach crowd 46–47
    wharf 26
    See also Port Hueneme
Hueneme Fisheries Company fishing dock, Port Hueneme 52
Hueneme Recreation Center 35
Hueneme wharf 26
Hueneme Wharf and Warehouse Company 52
Huffaker, M. E. 33
Hunt-Salto Canyon for dam destruction scene in "The Real Glory" 40
Hyland, Bill 126

I

Inadomi, Manuel 107
Inadomi Store, Oxnard 57, 107
Inouye, Mr. S. 137
Iverson, Ted 7
Iverson home, Torrey Hill, Piru 7
Iwamoto, Mr. K. 137
Iwamoto, Mr. M. 137

J

Jack Rose Smart Shop, Ventura 60
Japanese-Americans
    442nd Regimental Combat Team 105
    and Buddhist Church of Oxnard 75, 137
    Papa Shima mending anchovy nets 51
    relocation camps 5, 106–8
Japanese submarine offshore from Ellwood oil field, Santa Barbara 30
J.C. Penney store, Ventura 61
Jenkins, Rev. J.W. 74
Joe Andrade's Garage, Ventura 58, 68
Johnson's Radio Service sound car 129
Jungleland (Goebel's Lion Farm) Thousand Oaks 39, 40, 41

K

Kaiser, Bill 106
Klesira, Tony 126
Kolberg, Eric 128
Konamori, Mr. J. 137
Krishnamurti lectures 75
Kubota, Mr. and Mrs. 137
KVEN Studios, Pierpont Bay 67

L

labor unions 47
Lagomarsino, John 22
Lake Glenn Girl Scout Camp 78
Lakota Warrior (Stuart) 4
Lambeck, Arnie 126
Lamp, Ray 128
Lang, Don 128
Larrabee Stadium, Ventura 64, 102
Ledesma, Salvador 57
Leeds, Andrea 38
lemon orchards 33
Lewis, John C. *(Rain on Bellas Artes)* 4

Libbey Park, Ojai Valley Tennis Tournament at 125, 128
Life photographer for lighthouse move 23
lightning design on Chumas basket 4
lima beans
    bean planting tractor 35
    bean threshing 6–7
    conventions in Ventura County 34
    income from 33
    lima bean toast from Bill Baker's Bakery 51
Lincoln School, Ventura 73
Lindenbaum's Emporium, Oxnard 60
lions from Goebel's Lion Farm 39, 40, 41
L.N. Diedrich Machine Shop, Oxnard 60
Lorenzana, Joe 127
Louis, Joe 129
Lovatt, Art 106
Lovatt, Art K., Jr. 127
Luster Fish (Wood) 4
Lyons Pool 148

M

MacIssac, Don 127
March 1938 storms and floods
    bridge between Fillmore and Santa Paula destroyed twice 88
    evacuation of Ojai Valley and Santa Paula 88
    Railroad Bridge at Santa Paula 90–91
    road work needed after 87, 88
    Roosevelt Highway underpass crossing north of Oxnard 87
    Santa Paula Airport 89
    Santa Paula Creek Highway Bridge 91
    Saticoy Bridge washed out 91
    Seaside Oil tank farm surrounded by Ventura River 93
    Ventura River Flood of 1905 compared to 85
    Willard Bridge at Santa Paula 89
Margaret Schafer (vessel) 21
Maricopa Highway
    ban of highway billboards on 19
    completion of 16
    Days of the Golden West 1849 Boosters
        driving to Ventura on 139, 140
    opening celebration 19
    scenery from 17, 18, 19
Marquez, Phil 127
Marsh, Howard E. 72
Marshall, Delee Staunton 78
"M*A*S*H*" filming in eastern Ventura County 44
Masonic Lodge, Ventura 82
Masunaga, Rev. Taiken, and family 75
Matilija Canyon work camp 8
Matilija Dam, destruction of Lyons Pool for 148
Matilija Dam controversy 27
Matilija fire 93
Matilija Lake, Camp Edna Girl Scout Camp at 76
Matsumoto, Hisao 105
May Henning School, Ventura 73, 74
maypole dance on athletic field, Oxnard High School 70–71
McFarland, Bonita 34
McFarland Drive and Ventura Avenue fire 98
McFarland Ranch, Oxnard 34
McKenzie, Mrs. Don 20
Mears, Harold 128
Meiners Oaks Camp 92
"Men Into Space" (television series) 45
Merriam, Frank F. 8

Methodist Church, Moorpark...76
Mexican farm laborers...33
Meyers, Charles...65
Meyers' Bakery, Oxnard...65
military use of Ventura's beaches...115
Mira Loma Flight Academy, Oxnard Airport...110
Missourians reunion in Foster Park...137
Montoya, Ray...128
Moorpark
    Elliott Hendry Ranch apricot harvest...37
    Highway 118 at Moorpark intersection...150
    Methodist Church...76
Morgan, Dick...126
Moriwaki, Mr. T...137
movie industry...38–45
    and eastern Ventura County...44
    and Goebel's Lion Farm, Thousand Oaks...39, 40, 41
    and Point Mugu...45
    retrospective...39
    and Seaside Park, Ventura...39, 130
    Tarzan filming...40, 44
movies, filming of
    "A Few Good Men"...45
    "After the Sunset"...45
    "All Quiet on the Western Front"...44
    "The Crowd Roars"...39
    "Esquadrille"...45
    "High, Wide and Handsome"...41
    "North to Alaska"...45
    "The Real Glory"...38, 40, 42, 43
    "Road to Morocco"...41
    "A Yank in the Philippines"...43
Muni, Paul...45
mural in Ventura Post Office...13
Murray, Don...126
Museum of Ventura County
    about...4
    oral history of Goebel's Lion Farm...40
    Pioneer Monument...78–79

N

Nava, John...4
Naval Air Missile Test Center, Point Mugu...5
Naval Construction Battalion Center, Port Hueneme...110, 111
Navy band...119
Navy Radio Compass Station...110
Neal, Carl...128
Neilson, Deerheart...128
Neilson, Jo...45
Newbury Park
    snow scene...85
    Stagecoach Inn...145
Nicholson, Jack...45
Niven, David...38
Nixon, Richard M...123
Noah, Charlie...126
Noren, Len...126
Northrup, Walter...41
"North to Alaska" (movie)...45
Norton, Gwen...148
Norton, Marjorie...148
nudist colony opening prevented by Baptists...74

O

Oak View, Chismahoo Ranch west of...146
Oak View volunteer firefighters...123
ocean sports
    fishing...10, 11, 131
    sailing...131
Office of War Information...43
oil industry...28–31
    aerial view of oil fields...28–29
    the Avenue oil field...29, 30, 91, 92
    during Great Depression...7
    oil workers...62
    retrospective on...29
    and Ridge Route and Maricopa Highway projects...16
    Seaside Oil tank farm surrounded by Ventura River...93
    wire line bit for drilling, invention of...30–31
Ojai
    American Red Cross chapter...101
    Arya Vihara estate near...75
    Bill Baker's Bakery...49, 50, 51
    Boys Club...83
    fire station...8
    Foothills Hotel, original and rebuilt...54
    golf course converted to camp for soldiers...119
    Good Bread delivery trucks...51
    horse race in...125
    The Hub, Ojai...66
    ice cream parlor, bakery, and justice of the peace...67
    Main Street with a dusting of snow...152–53
    the Pergola...152–53
    tennis tournament in...125, 128
Ojai Arcade...143
Ojai Fire Station as work relief project...8
Ojai Good Bread delivery trucks...51
Ojai Maricopa fire...93
Ojai Valley Inn golf course converted to camp for soldiers...119
Ojai Valley Tennis Tournament, Libbey Park...125, 128
Older Girls Conference of Southern California, Ventura...131
Old Temescal School, Piru Canyon...73
Oliver, Cecilio...136
Olivet Baptist Church choir, Ventura...74
Oxnard
    aerial views...35, 36
    Army Air Corps cadets training in...110
    Asahi Market...107
    B and Fifth Streets...150
    beet sugar factory...35, 36
    Buddhist Church of Oxnard...75, 137
    Carnegie Library, Oxnard...129
    Crystal Brand Sugar...36
    Hollywood by-the-sea...45
    Inadomi Store, Oxnard...107
    Joe Louis's visit to...129
    Lindenbaum's Emporium...60
    L.N. Diedrich Machine Shop...60
    McFarland Ranch...34
    Meyers' Bakery...65
    Oxnard Boulevard businesses...61
    Oxnard Creamery...68
    parade on 5th Street...139
    Peoples Lumber Company...63
    Plaza Park...147
    Santa Clara Church...136
    scenic views of...35, 36, 150, 151, 153
    silo in...34
    St. Paul Baptist Church choir...74
    vegetable harvest...34
    Ventura County Ice...68
    women stretching on the beach...47
Oxnard Airport
    dedication...27
    Mira Loma Flight Academy at...110
Oxnard Boulevard businesses...61
Oxnard Canners Inc., Port Hueneme...53
Oxnard Citrus Association building...35
Oxnard Creamery...68
Oxnard Harbor District...22, 146
Oxnard High School maypole dance on athletic field...70–71

P

P-38 crash in upper Tapo Canyon...98
Pacific Coast Highway
    construction of...19
    opening of Coast Road from Oxnard...19
    sea wall at Point Mugu...20
Pacific Telephone, Ventura...63
Pacific Telephone and Telegraph Company, Ventura...63
Palo-Kangas, John...8
Palo-Kangas, Mrs...8
Pasadena Tournament of Roses parade float, Ventura...135
Paul, Joe, Jr....7
Peirano, Joe...127
Peirano, Ruby Bounds...101, 109
Peoples Lumber Company, Oxnard...63
the Pergola, Ojai...152–53
Peters, Chick...127
Petit, Allen...127
Petit, Helen Abplanalp...20
Peverley, Dora...20
Piedra Blanca work camp...8
Pierpont Bay
    cars lined up near...48
    KVEN studios in...67
    scenic view of...12
Pierpont Beach
    aerial view of Ventura from...144
    December 1937 high seas...99
    scenic of...48
Pierpont Inn, Delta Theta Tau Sorority installation held at...81
Pierpont pier
    destruction of...99
    fishing from and destruction of...97
Pinkerton, Edwin...121
Pinkerton, Roy...101, 116
Pioneer Monument at Foster Park near Casitas
    Springs dedication ceremony...78–79
Pioneer Picnic, Foster Park...137
Piru Canyon, Old Temescal School...73
Piru work camp...8
plane crashes due to pilots in training...98
Plaza Park, Oxnard...147
Plaza School, Ventura...73
Point Hueneme Lighthouse
    moving crew...24

preparation for moving ... 22, 23
reason for moving ... 23
view from the water ... 23
on the water ... 25
Point Mugu
   anchovies at ... 51
   Calleguas Creek Bridge construction ... 27
   "Esquadrille" filming in ... 45
   fish camp ... 95
   "Men Into Space" filming in (television series) ... 45
   new pier ... 95
   old pier with high surf ... 94, 95
   sailing at ... 131
   Santa Paula Aero class and Ventura County Grand Jury visit to ... 82
   "The Real Glory" filming at ... 40, 42, 43
Point Mugu Naval Air Missile Test Center ... 123
police and police departments
   California Highway Patrol ... 72
   motorcycles for ... 72
   retrospective ... 71
   Ventura Police Boys Club ... 126, 127, 129, 134
   Ventura Police personnel ... 71
Port Hueneme
   aerial photograph ... 15, 35, 147
   American Sailor docking at ... 20
   dedication celebration ... 22
   fishing boats at ... 52
   groundbreaking and dedication of ... 15
   harbor construction ... 14
   Harbor Days beauty queen contestants ... 20
   Hueneme Fisheries Company fishing dock ... 52
   Margaret Schafer docking at ... 21
   Naval ships in ... 104–5, 120–21
   news blackout during WWII ... 101
   Officers' Club in Bard Mansion ... 123
   Oxnard Canners Inc. ... 53
   pile driver in the dock area ... 119
   site of proposed harbor ... 15
   snowfall in ... 86
   U.S. Naval Advance Base Depot ... 113
   U.S. Navy supplies stored in ... 112
   wooden training boat ... 109
   during WWII ... 104–5
Port Hueneme wharf
   ship and sacks of cargo ... 20
Portland Beavers ... 125
Portuguese Crown Club Queen Virginia Faria ... 136
post offices
   Santa Paula, as work relief project ... 7
   Ventura, Grant's mural project in ... 13
postwar planning group ... 123
post-WWII expansion ... 5
POW camp for Germans ... 116
public services ... 70–83
   California Highway Patrol ... 72
   Camp Edna Girl Scout Camp, Matilija Lake ... 76
   Casa de Rosas Club ... 77
   Delta Theta Tau Sorority installation, Pierpont Inn ... 81
   fire station groundbreaking ... 81
   fleet of buses ... 64
   Lake Glenn Girl Scout Camp ... 78
   Oak View volunteer firefighters ... 123

Ojai Fire Station ... 8
regional Boy Scout meeting ... 81
retrospective ... 71
Santa Paula Aero class and Ventura County Grand Jury visit to Point Mugu ... 82
Santa Paula Fire Station ... 7
Twentieth Century Onyx Club ... 78
20-30 Club meeting ... 80
Ventura County Free Library Bookmobile ... 73
Ventura County Library story hour ... 83
work relief projects during Great Depression ... 7, 8, 13, 81
YWCA ... 82
See also police and police departments

Q
Queen Parade at Portuguese Crown Hall ... 136

R
racetrack, Ventura County Fairgrounds ... 130
Railroad Bridge at Santa Paula during March 1938 floods ... 90–91
Rain on Bellas Artes (Lewis) ... 4
"The Real Glory" (movie) ... 38, 40, 42, 43
Red Cross ... 101, 109
relaxation. *See* enjoyment and relaxation
religions
   Arya Vihara estate near Ojai ... 75
   Buddhist Church of Oxnard ... 75, 137
   Congregational Church, Ventura ... 74
   and diversity of population ... 71, 75
   Father Serra Cross reenactment ... 134
   First Baptist Church, Ventura ... 74
   Krishnamurti lectures ... 75
   Masonic Lodge, Ventura ... 82
   Methodist Church, Moorpark ... 76
   Olivet Baptist Church choir, Ventura ... 74
   San Buenaventura Mission sesquicentennial and tree-planting ceremony ... 133, 134, 135
   Santa Clara Church, Oxnard ... 136
   St. John's Seminary ... 75
   St. Paul Baptist Church choir, Oxnard ... 74
Research Library, Museum of Ventura County ... 4
retrospectives
   agricultural industry ... 33
   community services ... 71
   enjoyment and relaxation ... 125
   facing WWII ... 101
   on Great Depression ... 7
   on growth of the county ... 15, 47
   movie industry ... 39
   on oil industry ... 29
Riave, Max ... 66
Ridge Route redesign project ... 16
"Road to Morocco" (movie) ... 41
road work
   after March 1938 storms ... 87
   on coastline ... 19, 20
   on Maricopa Highway ... 16, 19
   on Ridge Route ... 16, 17
Robertson, Don Louie ... 131
Roe, Ralph ... 71
Rololand, Huren ... 127
Roosevelt Highway underpass crossing north of Oxnard after March 1938 storms ... 87

Rose Hotel, Ventura ... 53
Rose Parade, Pasadena ... 135
Rotsler, Lavelle ... 136
Russell Ranch, Conejo Valley ... 44
Ruth, Babe ... 126

S
sailing ... 131
Sakeda, Dick ... 57
San Buenaventura Mission sesquicentennial and tree-planting ceremony ... 133, 134, 135
Sandoz, Mr. ... 128
Sanhammer, Ralph ... 126
Santa Clara Church, Oxnard ... 136
Santa Clara River Valley March 1938 floods ... 88
Santa Paula
   evacuation of Ojai Valley and ... 88
   fire station and post office as work relief projects ... 7
   lemon packing house interior ... 32–33
   March 1938 storms washout bridge between Fillmore and ... 88
   Railroad Bridge during March 1938 floods ... 90–91
   Willard Bridge during March 1938 floods ... 89
Santa Paula Aero class ... 82
Santa Paula Airport ... 26, 27, 89
Santa Paula Band joins 1849 Boosters in Taft ... 140
Santa Paula Creek Highway Bridge during March 1938 floods ... 91
Santa Paula Hospital ... 77
Saticoy, Yeto Market ... 107
Saticoy Bridge washed out in March 1938 floods ... 91
schools and education
   Lincoln School, Ventura ... 73
   May Henning School, Ventura ... 73, 74
   Old Temescal School, Piru Canyon ... 73
   Oxnard High School maypole dance ... 70–71
   Plaza School, Ventura ... 73
   Ventura Junior College, Ventura ... 73
   Ventura Junior College Band, Ventura ... 135
   Ventura School crossing sign ... 72
   Ventura Union High School ... 125
   Willow School ... 4
   See also Ventura High School
Schumacher, William ... 127
Seabees
   activities in Ventura County ... 100–103
   band ... 102, 103
   equipment on the docks ... 113
   in formation on depot parade grounds ... 118
   parade through Ventura ... 100–101
   training at Advance Base Depot in Port Hueneme ... 110, 111, 113–15, 118
   war bond fund raising ... 100–103
   See also Advance Base Depot, Port Hueneme
seafood industry during Great Depression ... 11
Seaside Oil Company refinery, Ventura ... 91, 92
Seaside Oil tank farm surrounded by Ventura River ... 93
Seaside Park, Ventura
   Babe Ruth Field ... 126
   lima bean growers barbecue ... 34
   movie industry and ... 39, 130
   picnic and barbecue ... 137
   racehorses quartered in ... 130
   on racehorses quartered in ... 130
   Ventura Sons and Daughters of the

American Legion Fife, Drum and Bugle Corps ... 141
Seaward Avenue, Ventura ... 99, 146
Selby, Mark ... 11
Senõr Canyon (now Senior Canyon) backfire during Ojai-Maricopa Fire ... 93
Serra, Father Junipero ... 8
Serra Cross reenactment ... 134
Serra statute ... 8, 13
Seward Avenue bluff wind damage ... 99
Shell Oil employees ... 30
Sherwood Forest, filming of "All Quiet on the Western Front" in ... 44
Sherwood Lake ... 40
Shettle, M.L., Jr. ... 110
Shima, Papa ... 51
Shiozaki, Mr. T. ... 137
silo in Oxnard ... 34
Silva, Evelyn ... 136
Silva, Frank, Jr. ... 136
Silva, Sadi ... 136
Silveira, Johnnie ... 136
Siquedo, Richard ... 69
Smith, Harley ... 106, 127
Smith, Mrs. Fred W. ... 82
SNJ-type aircraft crash landing site ... 98
snowfall
in Bardsdale and Fillmore ... 85
at Newbury Park ... 85
in Ojai ... 152–53
in Port Hueneme ... 86
in Ventura ... 86, 87
softball, Ventura Police Boys Club team ... 127
Somis–Camarillo 4-H Club members on float for Ventura street fair ... 134
Somis work camp ... 8
Sorem, Bob ... 128
Sousa, Barbara ... 136
South Mountain, Texas Company Well #15 on Willard Lease on ... 30
Souza, Joe ... 45
Spalding, Wyman ... 123
sports. *See* enjoyment and relaxation
St. John's Seminary, between Camarillo and Somis ... 75
St. Paul Baptist Church choir, Oxnard ... 74
Stagecoach Inn, Newbury Park ... 145
Standard Plant No. 4 ... 30
The Star, 1920s
on economic prosperity in Ventura County ... 7
on movie making in Triunfo Canyon ... 44
on oil production ... 29
telephone hookups in Ventura ... 63
The Star, 1930s
ban of highway billboards on Maricopa Highway ... 19
Bill Baker's Bakery sends 100-pound fruitcake to the White House ... 49
bringing together jobless men and jobs (1930) ... 7
on celebration of Maricopa–Ventura Highway ... 15
on circus as aid to church fund ... 41
on completion of Conejo Pass ... 16
on Cuban sharks off Ventura wharf ... 11
on Disabled American Veterans Convention hotel room shortage ... 141
on elephants parading down the highway ... 40
on "Esquadrille" filming and weather problems ... 45
on farm yields ... 33
on Father Junipero Serra ... 8
on fire at Peoples Lumber Company ... 63
on harbor groundbreaking ceremonies ... 15
on highway from Ventura to New Hampshire ... 16
on Hotel Anacapa destruction plans ... 13
illiteracy decreasing ... 83
on income from movies ... 39
on John Quincy Adams's work at work relief program camp ... 8
man steals electricity from Father Serra Cross ... 134
on March 1938 floods ... 87, 88, 89, 90
on military's use of Ventura's beaches for training exercises ... 115
"Monster "V" Put on Hill" ... 125
on movie making in Seaside Park ... 39
nudist colony opening prevented by Baptists ... 74
on Oxnard Airport ... 27
on Pierpont Beach December 1937 high seas ... 99
on piers smashed by December 1937 storm ... 97
on plans for county seminary ... 75
Plaza School pupils move to new Lincoln school ... 73
on racehorses quartered in Seaside Park ... 130
on Santa Paula Airport ... 27
on teachers' pay increase ... 73
on Ventura County's strategic location for invaders ... 115
Ventura River Flood compared to 1938 storms ... 85
on waning of the Great Depression ... 47
on windstorm damage ... 99
The Star, 1940s
on Babe Ruth's visit ... 126
on battle of the lighthouse move ... 25
on farm labor and seasonal workers ... 33
on fire at Goebels ... 41
Navy provides a tour of Port Hueneme ... 113
on need for women to join the work force ... 116
on postwar planning group ... 123
Progress Edition ... 29, 47, 63, 77, 83
on promise of 1946 as the year "we've been waiting for" ... 101
results of war bond fund drives ... 103
Ventura County Fair attendance ... 9
The Star, 1980s, on Lion Farm trainer, Walter Northrup ... 41
State Highway Commission Ridge Route redesign ... 16
State Super Market, Ventura ... 61
Steele, Bob ... 128
stock market crash (1929), effect of ... 7
Stone, Lyman ... 126
Strobel, Beulah ... 148
Strobel, Jackie ... 148
Strobel, Johnny ... 148
Stroble, Bob ... 127
Stuart, George *(Lakota Warrior)* ... 4
Sturman, Johnny ... 126
Susuki, Takeo "Chick" ... 105, 106, 127
Suytar, Ellsworth ... 127
Suytar, Junior ... 127
Sycamore Cove, filming in ... 45

T

Taft, Santa Paula Band joins 1849 Boosters in ... 140
Takasugi, Abe ... 106, 107
Takasugi, George ... 108
Takasugi, Knox ... 108
Takasugi, Leonard ... 105, 106, 108
Takasugi, Nao ... 106, 107
Takasugi, Teno Kenmotsu ... 108
Takasugi, Thomas ... 108
Takeda, M. ... 137
Tarzan filming ... 40, 44
Taylor, Warren ... 127
Texas Company Well #15 on Willard Lease on South Mountain ... 30
Thousand Oaks, Goebel's Lion Farm ... 39, 40, 41
Thrift, Gene ... 106
Tierney, Cookie Timberlake ... 20
Tierney, Glen ... 20
Timberlake, Cookie ... 20
Topper Night Club, Ventura ... 67
tow truck at Joe Andrade's Garage, Ventura ... 58
transportation
buses lined up at Larrabee Stadium ... 64
of lions and elephants ... 40
motorcycles for police ... 72
Yellow Cab Company ... 66
See also automobiles and trucks
trucks. *See* automobiles and trucks
Twentieth Century Onyx Club ... 78
20-30 Club meeting ... 80

U

Universal Studios ... 41
Upham, Marilyn ... 59
U.S. Naval Advance Base Depot. *See* Advance Base Depot, Port Hueneme
"U.S. Naval Air Stations of World War II" (Shettle) ... 110
USS Oscar Badger ... 123

V

Valla, Gene ... 126
Van Dellen, Dan ... 128
Vanegas, Edward ... 128
Van Esse, Mr. ... 8
vegetable harvest in Oxnard ... 34
Ventura
the Avenue oil field ... 29, 30, 91, 92
Bard Sanitarium ... 77
bathhouse ... 56, 57
bond rallies in ... 100–101, 102
City Hall ... 8, 146
Congregational Church ... 74
courthouse ... 56
Grant Park ... 135
Larrabee Stadium ... 64
Masonic Lodge ... 82
McFarland Drive and Ventura Avenue fire ... 98
Older Girls Conference of Southern California ... 131
Olivet Baptist Church choir ... 74
Pasadena Tournament of Roses parade float ... 135
Seabees parade ... 100–101
Serra statute ... 8, 13
Somis–Camarillo 4-H Club members on float for street fair ... 134
Ventura County Hospital ... 77
Ventura pier ... 11, 97
Ventura Police Boys Club ... 126, 127, 129, 134
Ventura Post Office, Grant's mural project in ... 13
Ventura wharf ... 11, 57
Ventura Yankees baseball team ... 126
See also Days of the Golden West celebration; Seaside Park; Ventura businesses; Ventura scenic views; Ventura schools
Ventura Beach
aerial looking west from ... 142–43

Ventura County: Growing a County 159

military use of 115
scenics of 48
Ventura businesses
   Al. G. Wilson Dynamometer Service 64
   Coca-Cola Bottling Company 59
   DeLeon Hotel destruction 53
   General Machine Company 98
   Hotel Anacapa 13
   Hotel Ventura 150
   Jack Rose Smart Shop 60
   J.C. Penney store 61
   Joe Andrade's Garage 58, 68
   Pacific Telephone 63
   Rose Hotel 53
   Seaside Oil Company refinery 91
   State Super Market 61
   Topper Night Club 67
   Ventura Pipe and Construction Company 55
   Ventura Pistol Range 7, 81
   Ventura Sportswear Factory 66
   Ventura Theater at Chestnut and Main 53
   Ventura Wharf and Warehouse Company pier fire 84–85, 86
   Wonder Springs Water Company, Ventura 58
Ventura City Hall 8, 146
Ventura County bond rallies 100–103
Ventura County Boys Club 135
Ventura County Braves baseball team 124–25
Ventura County Courthouse
   city offices in 146
   employees in Days of the Golden West costumes 138
   Serra statue placed in front of 8
Ventura County Fair (1930) 9
Ventura County Fair (1940) 9
Ventura County Fairgrounds
   as Camp Seaside during WWII 30
   harness racing 130
   racetrack 130
Ventura County Free Library Bookmobile 73
Ventura County Grand Jury 82
Ventura County Hospital 77
Ventura County Ice, Oxnard 68
Ventura County Library story hour 83
Ventura County Missourians Society 137
Ventura County Parade 134
Ventura County YWCA 82
Ventura High School
   champion football team 128
   Ventura County League 1937 basketball team champions 127
   as Ventura Junior College, a work relief project 7
   visiting Fred Hall at KVEN Studios 67
Ventura Junior College, Ventura 73
Ventura Junior College Band, Ventura 135
Ventura pier 11, 97
Ventura Pistol Range, as work relief project 7, 81
Ventura Police Boys Club
   baseball team 126
   boxing match between 9-year-olds 129
   marching unit 134
   softball team 127
Ventura Post Office, Grant's mural project in 13
Ventura River
   artillery set up near for WWII security 30

during March 1938 storms 91, 92
Seaside Oil tank farm surrounded by 93
Ventura scenic views
   aerial from Pierpont Beach 144
   aerial looking west from the beach 142–43
   aerial of Seaside Park 130
   aerial view of oil fields 28–29
   aerial view pre-Highway 101 56–57
   California and Main Streets flooded 96
   Cedar Street onto Wall Street 144
   Main Street between California and Oak Streets 150
   Main Street looking west from Fir Street 144
   Main Street looking west toward Seaward Avenue 146
   Poli Street looking south, at night 149
   Seaward Avenue 99, 146
   snowfall 86, 87
   Ventura Avenue after flood 97
   of Ventura Beach 48, 142–43
   wharf and tracks 57
Ventura schools
   Lincoln School 73
   May Henning School 73, 74
   Plaza School 73
   Ventura Junior College 73
   Ventura Junior College Band 135
   Ventura School crossing sign 72
   Ventura Union High School 125
   See also Ventura High School
Ventura Sons and Daughters of the American Legion Fife,
   Drum and Bugle Corps at Seaside Park, Ventura 141
Ventura Sportswear Factory, Ventura 66
Ventura Union High School 125
Ventura wharf 11, 57
Ventura Wharf and Warehouse Company pier fire 84–85, 86
Ventura Yankees baseball team 126
Vorbeck, J.C. 131

W

Walker, Rev. Jesse 74
war bond drives 100–103
Watarida, Mr. S. 137
Wayne, John 45
weather
   heavy seas 85, 94, 95, 97, 98
   snowfall 85, 86, 87, 152–53
   windstorm damage 99, 134
   See also March 1938 storms and floods
Weatherley, Roy 66
Webster, Bob 126
Weed, Miss Myrna 82
Weed, Mrs. Nelson 82
Weigle, Violette 148
Wheeler Hot Springs 93, 148
Whitlock, Frank 45
Wigton, Jack 127
Willard Bridge at Santa Paula during March 1938 floods 89
Willard Lease on South Mountain, Texas Company Well #15 on 30
Williams, Leroy 106
Willow School children grinding acorns 4
Wilson, Archie 126
Wilson, Frank 106, 127
Wilson, Jack 106

windstorm damage 99, 134
Withers, Jack 128
women join the work force 116–17
Women's Army Corp (WACs) 109
women stretching on the beach, Oxnard 47
Wonder Springs Water Company, Ventura 58
Wood, Beatrice (Luster Fish) 4
Woolley, Clyde 128
work camps 8
work relief projects during Great Depression 7, 8, 13, 81
World War I movie, "All Quiet on the Western Front" 44
World War II 100–123
   442nd Regimental Combat Team 105
   Army Air Corps cadets training in Oxnard 110
   attack on Ellwood oil field north of Santa Barbara 30
   bond rallies in Ventura County 100–103
   Contractors Pacific Naval Air Bases Payroll Office 123
   effect of 5
   Japanese-Americans fighting in 442nd Regimental Combat Team 105
   Japanese-Americans in relocation camps 5, 106–8
   Japanese submarine offshore from Ellwood oil
     field, Santa Barbara 30
   Naval ships in Port Hueneme 104–5, 120–21
   Navy band 119
   Navy Radio Compass Station 110
   Ojai Valley Inn golf course converted to camp for soldiers 119
   plane crashes due to pilots in training 98
   Port Hueneme news blackout 101
   Port Hueneme Officers' Club in Bard Mansion 123
   postwar planning group 123
   POW camp for Germans 116
   retrospective 101
   security measures for Avenue oil field 30
   U.S. Navy supplies stored in Port Hueneme 112
   USS Oscar Badger 123
   women join the work force 116–17
   Women's Army Corp 109
   wooden training boat in Port Hueneme 109
   and "A Yank in the Philippines" (movie) 43
   See also Advance Base Depot, Port Hueneme; Seabees
worship. See religions

Y

Yamashita, Mr. Y. 137
"A Yank in the Philippines" (movie) 43
Yellow Cab Company 66
Yeto, Tomio 107, 137
Yeto, Utako 107
Yeto Market, Saticoy 107
Young, C.C. 19
YWCA, Ventura County 82

Z

Zaca fire in Santa Barbara and Ventura Counties 93